family circle®

Scones
& Muffins

The Family Circle® Promise of Success

Welcome to the world of Confident Cooking,
created for you in the Australian **Family Circle**®
Test Kitchen, where recipes are double-tested by
our team of home economists to achieve a
high standard of success—and delicious
results every time.

MURDOCH
B O O K S

Strawberry Shortcakes, page 19

Cheese Herb Scrolls, page 37

Capsicum and Corn Muffins, page 64

Krendl, page 71

Orange Berry Sponge, page 92

Passionfruit Butter Teacake, page 99

The Publisher thanks the following for their assistance in the photography for this book: Antico's Fruitworld, Phantasmagoria, Rinnai Australia, Ventura Design, Waterford Wedgwood.

Mixed Fruit Loaves, page 102

Chocolate Eclairs, page 83

The test kitchen, where our recipes are double-tested by our team of home economists to achieve a high standard of success and delicious results every time.

When we test our recipes, we rate them for ease of preparation. The following cookery ratings are on the recipes in this book, making them easy to use and understand.

A single Cooking with Confidence symbol indicates a recipe that is simple and generally quick to make – perfect for beginners.

Two symbols indicate the need for just a little more care and a little more time.

Three symbols indicate special dishes that need more investment in time, care and patience—but the results are worth it.

Front cover: Honey, date and ginger scones, page 18.

TIME FOR TEA

Teatime was once an important part of domestic life. In Victorian times, 'high tea' was an extravagant and formal affair that occurred every afternoon at four. Tea, of course, was served along with something savoury, such as cucumber or watercress sandwiches, and was followed by a teacake and several types of biscuits, or even a fancy gateau. Tea required not only a prodigious appetite, but many hours of preparation and preferably several servants. This type of occasion has disappeared with changing times, but there is no need for the traditional recipes, in all their delicious variety, to disappear as well. A piping hot batch of scones, for example, is a wonderful treat for hungry children home from school, or for an impromptu gathering of family and friends. Scones are quick and easy to make, requiring no special ingredients or equipment. They are delicious straight from the oven and, with a few imaginative toppings and fillings, can become a snack to remember. Savoury scones are perfect accompaniments to soups, stews and casseroles, as well as being delicious with tea or coffee.

Muffins, too, are exceptionally popular. The variety of ingredients, whether sweet or savoury, is almost limitless and, if anything, they are even easier to make than scones. Like scones, they are best eaten straight from the oven, while they are still warm, but they can be stored for several days in an airtight container, and are perfect for school lunches or to take on picnics.

Some of the other teatime treats we've included in this collection will require a little more skill and time than our scones and muffins, but are equally popular with crowds and are perfect for larger occasions, or for fetes and cake days.

Don't forget that well-made tea and coffee is vital to a successful tea party. Here are our tips for making the best possible refreshments.

The perfect cup of tea

Rinse a clean teapot with boiling water. Add about 1 teaspoon of loose, fresh tea leaves for each tea-drinker. (Only add the traditional 'one for the pot' if you like your tea strong.)

Bring plenty of cold fresh water to the boil, then add to the teapot immediately. Stir the brew once and leave to infuse for several minutes. (Tips will take about 3 minutes, whole leaves about 5 minutes.) Ideally, you should cover the teapot with a cosy to retain as much heat as possible. Strain tea into warmed cups or mugs.

Choose a tea that is likely to please most palates. The breakfast teas—Irish and English—are well liked as are the Indian teas, such as Darjeeling. China teas are very strong and fragrant (and purists will insist that they are served

with lemon, never milk) but are good for accompanying savoury dishes.

Herbal teas are not traditionally associated with teatime and may not suit everybody's taste buds or expectations. In hot weather you may wish to serve a large jug of iced tea as a refreshing thirst-quencher.

Milk—the burning question

Whether milk is introduced to the cup before or after the tea is usually a matter of preference and convenience. Technically, tea should have the milk added first, because the milk will scald slightly when it meets the hot tea and the whole brew will taste better. However, the difference may be indiscernible and may be impractical when catering for large groups. It may be better to offer a jug of milk and a dish of lemon slices alongside the pot and allow your guests to solve this dilemma themselves.

Coffee

Although a batch of scones is the traditional mark of a good cook, the ability to make a great cup of coffee is an equal challenge.

There are almost as many types of coffeemakers as there are blends of the coffee itself. Coffeemakers range from home cappuccino and espresso makers to drip-filter machines or simple plungers and percolators.

Whatever coffeemaker you use, you must complement it with a coffee that is ground specifically for that process. For example, finely ground coffee works best in forced-steam machines such as espresso or cappuccino makers. Medium ground coffee is best for plungers and filter-drip coffeemakers and coarsely ground coffee is needed for percolators or for steeping in a jug. In the case of the jug, you will need to strain the coffee well to remove the grounds. A specialist coffee shop or even a good delicatessen will be able

to advise you on which setting is best for your machine.

The vast choice of coffee bean flavours can make finding the right blend a bewildering, if tantalising, experience. The only way is to experiment—many good coffee shops will be willing to suggest all sorts of combinations for you; generally the darker the bean the more intense the flavour. (Some very dark beans may produce a bitter edge which is not to everyone's taste.) It is not a good idea to blend more than a few flavours at once, and some come in standard blends such as Mocha Kenya or Continental.

Buy coffee in quantities to last you two weeks only. Store in an airtight container in the refrigerator. If you are grinding your own, do so immediately before making the coffee.

TOPPINGS, FILLINGS JAMS AND BUTTERS

Scones, muffins and breads can be delicious on their own, but oozing with jam and cream or thickly spread with flavoured butter they make teatime a really special event.

LIQUEUR JAM

Put 1 cup apricot jam, 1 tablespoon Grand Marnier and 1 teaspoon finely grated orange rind in a pan. Stir over low heat for 2 minutes until well combined. Allow to cool.

HEALTHY FRUIT JAM

Combine 1/2 cup of sugar-free strawberry jam and 1 cup quartered strawberries in a small pan. Bring to the boil, reduce heat and simmer for 5–7 minutes or until berries have softened. Transfer to a bowl to cool.

LEMON CURD

Combine 3 egg yolks, 1/4 cup caster sugar, 50 g melted butter, 2 tablespoons lemon juice and 2 teaspoons finely grated lemon rind in a heatproof bowl. Whisk until sugar dissolves. Stand bowl over a pan of simmering water and stir constantly for 10 minutes until mixture thickens. Remove from heat. Transfer to a serving bowl to cool.

Anti-clockwise from top left: Liqueur Jam, Healthy Fruit Jam, Lemon Curd, Vanilla Passionfruit Cream, Choc-nut Cream, Sweet Yoghurt Cream, Berry Cream, Nutty Jam

NUTTY JAM

Spread ¼ cup slivered almonds on a baking tray and place in a 180°C oven for about 7 minutes or until lightly toasted. Cool completely, then stir into ½ cup fig jam.

BERRY CREAM

Using electric beaters, beat ⅔ cup cream with 2 tablespoons icing sugar until firm peaks form. Add 1 cup lightly crushed raspberries; swirl through gently with a metal spoon.

SWEET YOGHURT CREAM

Using electric beaters, beat ½ cup cream, 1 tablespoon of honey and 2 teaspoons grated orange rind until firm peaks form. Fold in ⅔ cup yoghurt with a metal spoon.

CHOC-NUT CREAM

Spread ½ cup pecans on an oven tray. Place in a 180°C oven for about 10 minutes or until lightly toasted; finely chop when cool. Beat 1 cup of cream until soft peaks form, then fold in chopped nuts and ⅓ cup grated dark chocolate.

VANILLA PASSIONFRUIT CREAM

Beat 1 cup cream with 2 tablespoons vanilla sugar until firm peaks form. Stir in ⅓ cup of passionfruit pulp.

GINGER PEAR COMPOTE

Combine $1/2$ cup water and $1/4$ cup sugar in a pan. Stir over low heat without boiling until sugar has dissolved. Peel, core and chop 2 large pears; add to pan with 2 tablespoons chopped glacé ginger. Bring to the boil, reduce heat and simmer uncovered for 10 minutes, until pears are soft and liquid has evaporated. Serve at room temperature.

SPICED MASCARPONE

Combine 1 cup mascarpone, 2 tablespoons maple syrup and $1/2$ teaspoon mixed spice. Beat briefly with electric beaters until thick; take care not to curdle by overbeating.

SPICED APPLE BUTTER

Peel, core and chop 3 cooking apples. Combine in a pan with 1 tablespoon lemon juice and 50 g butter. Cook, covered, over low heat 10 minutes or until soft. Add 1–2 tablespoons sugar and $1/2$ teaspoon each of cinnamon and mixed spice; stir well. Serve at room temperature.

RUMMY DATE SPREAD

Stone 250 g fresh dates, discard stones and finely chop the flesh. Place in a pan with 1 tablespoon rum, 25 g butter and $1/4$ cup water. Stir over heat for about 3 minutes or until soft and smooth.

Clockwise from bottom left: Ginger Pear Compote, Spiced Mascarpone, Spiced Apple Butter, Rummy Date Spread, Easy Berry Jam, Toffee Nut Cream, Brandy Cream, Hazelnut Cream

EASY BERRY JAM

Combine 300 g raspberries (fresh or thawed), 1 peeled and chopped apple and 2 tablespoons caster sugar in a pan. Bring to the boil (berries will become liquid as they heat), reduce heat and simmer, stirring occasionally, for about 20 minutes or until thick.

TOFFEE NUT CREAM

Line an oven tray with foil and brush lightly with oil. Sprinkle 1/4 cup sugar into a heavy-based pan; scatter with 1/4 cup blanched almonds. Cook over very low heat until sugar melts and turns golden. (Tilt pan slightly, if necessary, but do not stir.) Pour into tray and leave to set. Crush set toffee in food processor to fine crumbs; combine in a bowl with 1 cup pure thick cream. Stir to combine.

BRANDY CREAM

Combine 1/2 cup cream, 1/2 cup ready-made custard and 1 tablespoon of brandy in a bowl. Using electric beaters, beat until slightly thickened.

HAZELNUT CREAM

Using electric beaters, beat 2/3 cup cream to firm peaks. Add 1/4 cup choc-hazelnut spread and swirl through with a metal spoon or flat-bladed knife.

CITRUS BUTTER

Cut 125 g room-temperature butter into cubes; combine in a food processor with 1/4 cup honey, the grated rind of 1 orange, 1 tablespoon orange juice and 1/2 teaspoon cinnamon. Blend until smooth.

MIXED NUT BUTTER

Cut 125 g room-temperature butter into cubes; combine in a food processor with 150 g unsalted roasted mixed nuts and 2 teaspoons grated orange rind. Blend until smooth.

HONEY-PECAN BUTTER

Cook 1/3 cup pecans under a medium grill for 2–3 minutes until very lightly roasted. Cut 125 g butter into cubes and combine with pecans and 1/4 cup honey in a food processor. Blend until smooth.

STRAWBERRY BUTTER

Cut 125 g room-temperature butter into cubes and combine in a food processor with 1 tablespoon caster sugar and 1 cup chopped strawberries. Blend until smooth.

APRICOT BUTTER

Place 1/2 cup chopped dried apricots in bowl and cover with hot water; leave to soften 15 minutes. Drain and combine in food processor with 125 g room-temperature butter, cut into cubes, and 1 tablespoon caster sugar. Blend until smooth.

COOK'S FILE

Storage time: All flavoured butters can be stored, covered, in the refrigerator. Bring back to room temperature before serving. Butters can also be frozen for up to 1 month.

HERB BUTTER

Cut 125 g room-temperature butter into cubes and put in a food processor with 1/4 cup of chopped parsley, 1 tablespoon each of chopped basil and tarragon, 1 crushed clove of garlic and 1 teaspoon lemon juice. Blend until smooth.

MUSTARD BUTTER

Cut 125 g room-temperature butter into cubes and combine in a food processor with 1 tablespoon each Dijon and French mustards and 2 tablespoons finely chopped parsley. Blend until smooth.

SUN-DRIED TOMATO BUTTER

Drain and chop 1/3 cup oil-packed sun-dried tomatoes. Cut 125 g butter into cubes and combine in a food processor with the sun-dried tomatoes and 1 teaspoon lemon juice. Blend until smooth.

CHILLI BUTTER

Cut 125 g room-temperature butter into cubes and combine in a food processor with 1–2 small chopped red chillies, 2 tablespoons chopped fresh coriander and 1/2 teaspoon ground cumin. Blend until smooth.

HORSERADISH BUTTER

Cut 125 g room-temperature butter into cubes and combine in a food processor with 1 tablespoon horseradish cream, 1 tablespoon chopped chives and 1 teaspoon lemon juice. Blend until smooth.

From left: first column (from top): Citrus Butter, Mixed Nut Butter, Honey-Pecan Butter; second column: Strawberry Butter, Apricot Butter; third column: Herb Butter, Mustard Butter, Sun-Dried Tomato Butter; fourth column: Chilli Butter, Horseradish Butter

SCONES

HOW TO MAKE PERFECT SCONES

Making great scones is not difficult, and they get even easier with practice. This step-by-step guide will see you through the first few batches. First, read through the recipe and assemble all the ingredients, weighing and measuring carefully. Preheat the oven, prepare the baking tray by brushing it with melted butter or oil, then begin. All scones are made according to the same principles: add the wet ingredients to the dry and mix the dough as briefly and lightly as possible.

1 Sift the flour and any other dry ingredients into a large bowl. Sifting adds air to the flour which contributes to lighter scones. If you are using wholemeal flour, tip the husks back into the bowl for added texture. (It is still important to sift, however, as this aerates the flour.) Have the butter at room temperature and chop it into small pieces. Rub the butter into the flour briefly and lightly, using your fingertips, until fine and crumbly. The secret to light scones is a light touch.

2 Next, make a well in the centre of the dry ingredients and add almost all the liquid. The moisture content of flour can vary a great deal between brands, and even between different packets of the same brand, so you may not need all the liquid. Mix the liquid into the flour, using a knife in a quick cutting motion, rotating the bowl. (Using a knife rather than a wooden spoon helps not to overwork the dough.) The mixture will come together in small moist pieces. Mix in some more liquid if the dough is dry.

3 Gather the dough together and turn it out onto a clean, lightly floured surface. Use the flour suggested in the recipe (usually self-raising).

4 Knead the dough very lightly, folding it back over itself and pressing down; make a quarter turn and repeat the action. Knead for only about 30–40 seconds. The dough should have *just* lost its stickiness.

5 Roll or press the dough out to a flat round about 2 cm thick. Cut out rounds with a lightly floured scone cutter. Pile the scraps together and press or roll out; don't re-knead. Place the scones close together on the tray.

6 Glaze scones by brushing them with milk, or according to the recipe. Bake until well risen and golden on top. If you aren't sure they are cooked, break one open. If it is still doughy in the centre, cook for a few minutes more. For soft scones, wrap in a clean tea towel while still hot. For scones with a crisp top, transfer to a wire rack to cool slightly.

Storage: Scones are best eaten within a few hours but they can be frozen in a bag for up to 3 months.

Use your fingertips to rub the butter into the flour.

Add almost all the liquid ingredients and mix with a flat-bladed knife.

Gather the dough into a rough ball and transfer to the work surface.

Knead the dough lightly, folding it in over itself several times.

Re-roll the dough scraps, but do not knead again.

Brush the rounds with a little milk to glaze the tops.

Strawberry Shortcakes, page 19

PLAIN SCONES

Preparation time: 20 minutes
Total cooking time: 12 minutes
Makes 12

2 cups self-raising flour
pinch salt, optional (see Note)
30 g butter, cut into small
  pieces
1/2 cup milk
1/3 cup water
milk, extra, for glazing

1 Preheat oven to 210°C (190°C gas). Brush an oven tray with melted butter or oil. Sift the flour and salt (if using) into a bowl. Add the chopped butter and rub in lightly using your fingertips.
2 Make a well in the centre of the flour. Add almost all of the combined milk and water. Mix with a flat-bladed knife to a soft dough, adding more liquid if necessary.
3 Turn dough onto a lightly floured surface (use self-raising flour). Knead dough briefly and lightly until smooth. Press or roll out dough to form a round 1–2 cm thick.
4 Cut the dough into rounds using a floured round 5 cm cutter. Place rounds on prepared tray; glaze rounds with milk. Bake 10–12 minutes or until golden brown. Serve scones with jam and whipped cream.

COOK'S FILE

Note: Add a pinch of salt to your scones, even the sweet ones. Salt acts as a flavour enhancer and will not be tasted in the cooked product.

SULTANA SCONES

Preparation time: 20 minutes
Total cooking time: 12 minutes
Makes 12

2 cups self-raising flour
pinch salt
30 g butter, cut into small
    pieces
1/3 cup caster sugar
1/4 cup sultanas
1 egg, lightly beaten
3/4 cup milk
extra milk, for glazing

1 Preheat oven to 210°C (190°C gas). Brush an oven tray with melted butter or oil. Sift flour and salt into a large bowl. Add butter and rub in lightly with fingertips.

2 Add sugar and sultanas and stir to combine. Make a well in the centre of the mixture. Add egg and almost all the milk. Mix quickly, with a flat-bladed knife, to a soft dough, adding more milk if necessary. Turn out onto a lightly floured surface and knead briefly until smooth. Press or roll out to form a round about 2 cm thick.

3 Cut dough into rounds using a floured plain 5 cm cutter or cut into squares using a floured knife. Place scones close together on prepared tray and brush with extra milk. Bake for 10–12 minutes or until golden brown. Serve buttered.

COOK'S FILE

Variation: Use any type of dried fruit in this recipe, for example, currants, raisins, or chopped and pitted dates or prunes.

Add the sugar and sultanas and stir to combine with a wooden spoon.

CINNAMON SCROLLS

Preparation time: 25 minutes
Total cooking time: 12 minutes
Makes 12

2 cups self-raising flour
pinch salt
90 g butter, chopped
2/3 cup milk

Filling
60 g butter, softened
2 tablespoons soft brown sugar
1 teaspoon cinnamon

Icing
1 cup icing sugar, sifted
1 tablespoon boiling water

1 Preheat oven to 210°C (190°C gas). Brush an oven tray with melted butter or oil. Sift flour and salt into bowl. Rub butter into flour using your fingertips. Make a well in the centre; add almost all the milk. Mix lightly, with flat-bladed knife, to a soft dough, adding more liquid if necessary.
2 Knead dough briefly on a lightly floured surface until smooth. Roll out dough to a 25 x 40 cm rectangle of 5 mm thickness.
3 To make Filling: Using electric beaters, beat butter and combined sugar and cinnamon until light and fluffy. Spread evenly over the dough rectangle. Roll up the dough from the long side. Using a sharp knife, slice the dough into 3 cm pieces. Place dough pieces close together, cut-side up, on the prepared tray. Cook for 12 minutes or until golden. Remove from oven to cool slightly. Drizzle with Icing.
4 To make Icing: Combine icing sugar and boiling water in a small bowl. Beat mixture until smooth and well combined.

COOK'S FILE

Variation: Add chopped sultanas to Filling, if desired.

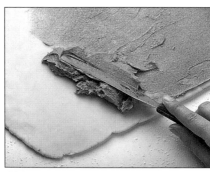

Using a flat-bladed knife, spread Filling evenly over dough.

Place the scrolls, close together, on the prepared tray.

SPICY FRUIT AND NUT SCONES

Preparation time: 20 minutes
Total cooking time: 10–12 minutes
Makes 12

2 cups self-raising flour
pinch salt
30 g butter, chopped
1 tablespoon caster sugar
1/2 cup chopped dried fruit
   medley
2 tablespoons finely chopped
   walnuts
1/4 teaspoon mixed spice
1/4 teaspoon ground ginger
1/4 teaspoon ground
   cloves
1/2 cup milk
1/4 cup water
milk, extra, for glazing

2 teaspoons caster sugar,
   extra
1/2 teaspoon cinnamon

1 Preheat oven to 210°C (190°C gas).
Brush an oven tray with melted butter
or oil. Sift flour and salt into bowl;
add butter and rub into flour. Add
caster sugar, dried fruit, walnuts,
mixed spice, ground ginger and
ground cloves; stir to combine. Make
a well in the centre.
2 Add almost all of the combined
milk and water to flour mixture. Mix
lightly, with a flat-bladed knife, to
form a soft dough, adding more liquid
if necessary.
3 Knead dough briefly on a lightly
floured surface until smooth; press
out dough to 2 cm thickness. Using a
floured 5 cm round cutter, cut rounds
from dough. Place rounds on the
prepared tray and brush with extra

milk. Combine caster sugar and
cinnamon and sprinkle over scones.
Cook for 10–12 minutes until golden
brown. Serve scones warm or cold
with butter.

COOK'S FILE

Variation: Omit cinnamon and sugar
topping, if preferred.

*Sprinkle the combined cinnamon and
caster sugar over the scones.*

HONEY, DATE AND GINGER SCONES

Preparation time: 25 minutes
Total cooking time: 15 minutes
Makes 12

1/2 cup fresh dates
1/4 cup glacé ginger
2 cups self-raising flour
1/2 teaspoon ground
    ginger
pinch salt
1 tablespoon honey
1/2 cup milk
1/4 cup cream

Honey Glaze
1 tablespoon milk
1 teaspoon honey

1 Preheat oven to 210°C (190°C gas). Brush an oven tray with melted butter or oil. Chop the dates and the glacé ginger into small chunks. Sift flour, ground ginger and salt into bowl; add dates and glacé ginger; stir to combine.

2 Combine honey, milk and cream in small pan and stir over low heat until well combined. Add to flour mixture and mix lightly, with a flat-bladed knife, to form a soft dough, adding more milk if necessary. (The dough should have just lost its stickiness but not become dried or tough.)

3 Knead dough briefly on a lightly floured surface until smooth and press out to 2 cm thickness. Cut rounds from dough with a floured plain 5 cm cutter. Place scones on prepared tray; brush dough with Honey Glaze. Cook 12–15 minutes or until lightly golden.

4 To make Honey Glaze: Gently warm milk and honey in a pan, stirring until well combined.

COOK'S FILE

Note: Use self-raising flour on your hands and work surfaces.

Chop the dates and the glacé ginger to desired size.

18

STRAWBERRY SHORTCAKES

Preparation time: 20 minutes
Total cooking time: 12 minutes
Makes 12

30 g butter
2 tablespoons caster sugar
1 egg
1½ cups self-raising flour
pinch salt
½ cup milk
1 tablespoon milk, extra
1 tablespoon caster sugar, extra
strawberries, halved, and whipped cream, for serving

1 Preheat oven to 210°C (190°C gas). Brush an oven tray with oil or melted butter. Using electric beaters, beat butter and sugar until light and fluffy. Add egg and mix well.
2 Sift the flour and salt into a bowl. Make a well in the centre; add butter, sugar and egg mixture and almost all of the milk. Mix lightly, with a flat-bladed knife, to a soft dough, adding more milk if necessary. Knead dough briefly on a lightly floured surface until smooth. Press out dough to 2 cm thickness. Using a floured plain 5 cm cutter, cut rounds from the dough and place on the prepared tray.
3 Brush rounds with extra milk and top with a sprinkling of caster sugar. Bake for 10–12 minutes or until lightly golden. When scones are cool, split and serve with strawberries and whipped cream.

COOK'S FILE

Note: Handle the scone mixture lightly. If the dough is over-mixed, it will become tough.

After creaming the butter and sugar, add the egg.

19

WHOLEMEAL DATE SCONES

Preparation time: 20 minutes
Total cooking time: 15 minutes
Makes 12

1¹/2 cups self-raising flour
1¹/2 cups wholemeal
    self-raising flour
¹/2 teaspoon baking powder
¹/4 teaspoon salt
60 g butter, cut into
    small pieces
2 tablespoons caster sugar
1 cup chopped dates
1¹/4 cups buttermilk
¹/2 cup water
buttermilk, extra,
    for glazing

1 Preheat oven to 210°C (190°C gas). Brush an oven tray with melted butter or oil. Sift the flours, baking powder and salt into a large bowl, returning the husks. Add the chopped butter and rub in lightly using your fingertips. Stir in the sugar and the chopped dates.

2 Make a well in the centre of the flour mixture. Add the buttermilk and almost all of the water. Mix quickly, using a flat-bladed knife, to form a soft dough, adding more water if necessary. (The dough should have lost its stickiness but not become dried or tough.)

3 Knead dough briefly on a lightly floured surface until smooth. Press out the dough with floured hands to form a 2 cm thick square. Cut into 16 smaller squares. Place the squares on the prepared tray, leaving a 2 cm gap between each scone. Brush with extra buttermilk.

4 Bake scones for 12–15 minutes or until golden brown. Serve warm with butter.

COOK'S FILE

Note: These are more heavily textured scones than the traditional recipe. Returning the flour husks to the mixture will contribute to this texture, however it is still necessary to sift the flours as this introduces air through the dry ingredients.

Variation: Use margarine in place of the butter, if you like.

Sift the self-raising flours into a large bowl, returning the husks.

Place dough squares on prepared tray, leaving a slight gap.

WHOLEMEAL APPLE SCONES

Preparation time: 20 minutes
Total cooking time: 25 minutes
Makes 8

1 cup wholemeal
   self-raising flour
1 cup self-raising flour
pinch salt
1½ teaspoons cinnamon
¼ cup soft brown sugar
1 green apple, peeled
   and grated
30 g butter, melted
½ cup skim milk
milk, extra, for glazing
1 tablespoon caster sugar,
   for sprinkling

1 Preheat oven to 210°C (190°C gas). Brush an oven tray with melted butter or oil. Sift flours, salt and 1 teaspoon cinnamon into a large bowl, returning the husks. Add the sugar and apple and stir until combined.

2 Make a well in the centre of the flour mixture. Add butter and almost all of the milk. Mix quickly with a flat-bladed knife to form a smooth dough, adding more milk if necessary.

3 Knead dough briefly on a lightly floured surface until smooth. Pat into a 20 cm round and place on prepared tray. Score dough into 8 even wedges, cutting almost all the way through. Brush with extra milk and sprinkle with sugar and remaining cinnamon. Bake 20–25 minutes or until golden brown. Slice into 8 portions when cool. Serve with butter.

COOK'S FILE

Note: The size and moisture content of the apple will dictate how much milk is needed to form a soft dough. Add the extra milk in very small amounts and try not to overwork the dough.

Score the uncooked dough round into eight wedges.

SOUR CREAM AND CURRANT SCONES

Preparation time: 10 minutes
Total cooking time: 10–15 minutes
Makes 12

2 cups self-raising flour
pinch salt
90 g butter, cut into small
   pieces
1/4 cup currants
2 tablespoons caster sugar
1/2 cup sour cream
1 egg, lightly beaten

1 Preheat oven to 210°C (190°C gas). Brush an oven tray with melted butter or oil. Sift flour and salt into a large bowl. Add butter and rub in using fingertips. Add currants and sugar and stir through. Make a well in the centre of the flour mixture. Add almost all the combined sour cream and egg. Mix quickly, with a flat-bladed knife, to a soft dough, adding more liquid if necessary. (The dough should have just lost its stickiness, but not become dried or tough.) Knead briefly on a lightly floured surface until smooth. Press or roll out to form a round about 2 cm thick.
2 Cut the dough into rounds using a floured 5 cm scone cutter. Place the rounds close together on prepared tray. Bake for 10–15 minutes or until scones are golden brown. Serve warm with butter.

COOK'S FILE

Variation: For a delicious and rich scone, add 60 g grated chocolate with sugar. You could also add 1/2 cup of chopped prunes, diced apricots, or ground almonds to the flour mixture.

CREAM SCONES

Preparation time: 15 minutes
Total cooking time: 12 minutes
Makes 8

2 cups self-raising flour
pinch salt
2 teaspoons caster sugar
30 g butter, cut into
   small pieces
3/4 cup cream
1/4 cup water

1 Preheat oven to 210°C (190°C gas). Brush an oven tray with oil or melted butter. Sift the flour and salt into a large bowl; add the sugar and stir thoroughly to combine. Add the butter and rub in lightly, using your fingertips.

2 Make a well in the centre of the flour. Add almost all of the combined cream and water. Mix quickly, using a flat-bladed knife, to form a soft dough, adding more liquid if necessary. (Reserve a teaspoon of cream mixture for glazing.)

3 Knead dough briefly on a lightly floured surface until smooth, but still slightly sticky. Press out dough with your hands to form a 2 cm thick round. Cut dough into 8 rounds using a floured plain 5 cm cutter. Arrange on prepared tray and brush scones with reserved cream mixture.

4 Bake 10–12 minutes or until golden brown. Transfer to a wire rack and cover with a clean tea towel to keep scones soft. Serve warm.

COOK'S FILE

Storage time: Cream Scones are best eaten on the day of baking.

BUTTERMILK SCONES

Preparation time: 15 minutes
Total cooking time: 10–12 minutes
Makes 12

2 cups self-raising flour
pinch salt
30 g butter
1 cup buttermilk
jam and whipped cream,
to serve

1 Preheat oven to 210°C (190°C gas). Brush oven tray with melted butter or oil. Sift the flour and salt into a large bowl; add chopped butter. Using your fingertips, rub the butter into the flour. Add almost all of the buttermilk. Mix lightly, with a flat-bladed knife, to a soft dough, adding more liquid if necessary. (The dough should have just lost its stickiness, but not become dried or tough.)

2 Knead briefly on a lightly floured surface until smooth. Press dough to 1 cm thickness. Cut dough into rounds with a floured 5 cm plain or fluted cutter. Place rounds close together on prepared tray. Bake 10–12 minutes or until golden brown. Serve scones warm with apricot or strawberry jam and softly whipped cream.

COOK'S FILE

Note: Buttermilk has a slightly sour, tangy taste. Its acid reacts with the self-raising flour, making the dough rise and is, thus, ideal for baking.

Left to right: Sour Cream and Currant Scones, Cream Scones, Buttermilk Scones

JAM PINWHEELS

Preparation time: 10 minutes
Total cooking time: 20 minutes
Makes about 12

2¹/2 **cups self-raising flour**
pinch salt
30 g butter, cut into
  small pieces
¹/3 **cup caster sugar**
²/3 **cup milk**
1 egg, lightly beaten
¹/3 **cup strawberry jam**
milk, for glazing

1 Preheat oven to 210°C (190°C gas).
Brush an 18 x 28 cm shallow tin with
oil or melted butter. Sift flour and salt
into a large bowl. Add butter and rub
in with your fingertips. Add the sugar
and stir it through. Make a well in the
centre of the flour mixture. Add
almost all of the combined milk and
egg. Mix lightly, with a flat-bladed
knife, to a soft dough, adding more
liquid if necessary. (Dough should
have just lost its stickiness, but not
become dried or tough.) Knead briefly
on a lightly floured surface. Roll out to
form a rectangle about 1 cm thick.
2 Warm jam in microwave or over
low heat. Spread over the dough. Roll
up from long side as for a Swiss roll.
Cut roll into 2 cm lengths.
3 Place dough cut-side up in prepared tin; brush dough with milk.
Bake for 15–20 minutes or until
golden brown. Turn onto a wire rack
to cool. Serve scones warm or cool
with butter or cream.

COOK'S FILE

Variations: Spread dough with fruit
mince instead of jam, if you prefer.

*Roll up dough from the long side as for a
Swiss roll.*

RASPBERRY BUN SCONES

Preparation time: 20 minutes
Total cooking time: 12 minutes
Makes 8

2 cups self-raising flour
pinch salt
2 tablespoons caster sugar
1/2 cup milk
30 g butter, melted
1/3 cup water
1 tablespoon raspberry jam
1 tablespoon milk, extra
caster sugar, extra

1 Preheat oven to 210°C (190°C gas). Brush an oven tray with melted butter or oil. Sift the flour and salt into a large bowl; add the sugar and stir to combine.

2 Make a well in the centre of the flour. Add combined milk and melted butter all at once, reserving a teaspoonful for glazing. Add almost all of the water. Mix quickly, using a flat-bladed knife, to form a soft dough, adding more water if necessary.

3 Knead dough briefly on a lightly floured surface until smooth. Cut dough into 8 rounds using a floured 7 cm cutter. Turn each scone over and make an indentation in the centre with your thumb; place 1/2 teaspoon of jam in indentation and fold over dough. Place scones, well apart, on prepared tray; flatten tops slightly. Brush with milk and sprinkle liberally with caster sugar. Bake for 10–12 minutes or until golden.

COOK'S FILE

Note: Any sweet jam can be used in this recipe.

Spoon jam into the indentation, then fold over the dough.

PUMPKIN SCONES

Preparation time: 35 minutes
Total cooking time: 12 minutes
Makes 12

30 g butter, chopped
2 tablespoons caster sugar
1/2 cup mashed cooked pumpkin
1 egg, lightly beaten
1/2 cup milk
2 1/2 cups self-raising flour
pinch salt
milk, for glazing

1 Preheat oven to 210°C (190°C gas). Brush an oven tray with melted butter or oil. Using electric beaters, beat the butter and sugar in a small bowl until the mixture is light and creamy. Add pumpkin, egg and milk and mix well.
2 Sift flour and salt into a large bowl. Make a well in the centre; add almost all of the pumpkin. Mix lightly with a flat-bladed knife to a soft dough, adding more liquid if necessary.
3 Knead dough briefly on a lightly floured surface. Press or roll out dough to 2 cm thickness.
4 Cut dough into rounds using a floured plain 5 cm cutter. Place scones, close together, on prepared tray. Brush with a little milk. Bake for 10–12 minutes until golden brown. Serve warm with butter.

COOK'S FILE

Note: To make 1/2 cup of mashed pumpkin you will need around 250 g of raw pumpkin.

Add the pumpkin, egg and milk and stir well with a wooden spoon.

MINI ONION AND PARMESAN SCONES

Preparation time: 25 minutes
Total cooking time: 8–10 minutes
Makes 24

30 g butter, chopped
1 small onion, finely chopped
2 cups self-raising flour, sifted
pinch salt
1/2 cup finely shredded parmesan cheese
1/2 cup milk
1/2 cup water
cayenne pepper, for sprinkling (optional)

1 Preheat oven to 210°C (190°C gas). Brush an oven tray with melted butter or oil. Melt butter in a small pan; add onion and cook, over low heat, 2–3 minutes or until soft; cool slightly.
2 Combine flour, salt and parmesan cheese in a bowl. Make a well in the centre; add onion and almost all the combined milk and water. Mix lightly, with a flat-bladed knife, to a soft dough, adding more liquid if necessary.
3 Knead the dough briefly on a lightly floured surface until smooth and press out to 2 cm thickness. Cut the dough into rounds with a floured 3 cm plain round cutter. Place rounds on the prepared tray and sprinkle each lightly with cayenne pepper, if using. Cook for 10–12 minutes until golden brown.

COOK'S FILE

Note: Be careful not to use too much flour when kneading or a tough, dry dough will result. Use self-raising flour for your hands and the work surface.

Add onion and cook over low heat until softened; cool before using.

HERB SCONES

Preparation time: 25 minutes
Total cooking time: 12 minutes
Makes 12

2 cups self-raising flour
1/2 teaspoon salt
30 g butter
1 tablespoon chopped
    fresh thyme
1 tablespoon chopped
    fresh parsley
1 tablespoon chopped
    fresh marjoram
1/2 cup milk
1/4 cup water
milk, extra, for glazing

1 Preheat oven to 210°C (190°C gas). Brush an oven tray with melted butter or oil. Sift flour and salt into large bowl. Rub butter into flour with your fingertips. Add herbs and stir to combine. Make a well in the centre of the mixture.
2 Add almost all of the combined milk and water to flour mixture; mix lightly with a flat-bladed knife to a soft dough, adding more liquid if necessary. Knead dough briefly on a lightly floured surface until smooth and roll out to 2 cm thickness.
3 Using a floured 5 cm plain round cutter, cut rounds from dough and place on prepared tray. Brush dough with extra milk and cook for 10–12 minutes. Serve with butter.

COOK'S FILE

Note: These scones will taste best when fresh herbs are used, however dried herbs can also be used. Use around a third of the fresh quantity.

Add chopped herbs after rubbing the butter into the flour.

CHEESE AND CHIVE SCONES

Preparation time: 20 minutes
Total cooking time: 12 minutes
Makes 9

2 cups self-raising flour
pinch salt
30 g butter
1/2 cup grated cheddar cheese
1/4 cup shredded parmesan
   cheese
2 tablespoons snipped chives

1/2 cup milk
1/2 cup water
1/4 cup grated cheddar cheese,
   extra

1 Preheat oven to 210°C (190°C gas). Brush an oven tray with melted butter or oil. Sift the flour and salt into bowl. Rub in butter using your fingertips. Stir in cheeses and the chives. Make a well in the centre; add the milk and almost all of the water. Mix lightly with a flat-bladed knife to a soft dough, adding more liquid if necessary.

2 Knead dough briefly on a lightly floured surface until smooth. Press out dough to 2 cm thickness. Using a floured 5 cm plain round cutter, cut rounds from dough. Place rounds on prepared tray and sprinkle with extra cheese. Cook for 12 minutes or until cheese is golden in colour.

COOK'S FILE

Hint: For crusty scones, allow them to cool, uncovered, on a wire rack. For softer scones, wrap them in a tea towel while they are still warm and leave to cool.

CURRY CRESCENT SCONES

Preparation time: 20 minutes
Total cooking time: 25 minutes
Makes 12

30 g butter
6 spring onions, finely
    chopped
2 teaspoons curry powder
1/3 cup parsley, finely
    chopped
1/2 cup cheddar cheese,
    grated
2 cups self-raising flour
1/4 teaspoon salt
1/2 cup milk
1/3 cup water
1 teaspoon milk, extra,
    for glazing
paprika, for sprinkling

1 Preheat oven to 210°C (190°C gas).
Brush an oven tray with melted butter
or oil. Melt butter in a small pan; add
spring onions and cook over low heat
5 minutes or until softened. Stir in
curry powder and remove pan from
heat. Mix in parsley and cheese.
2 Sift flour and salt into a large bowl.
Make a well in the centre. Add
the milk and almost all of the water.
Mix quickly, with a flat-bladed knife,
to a soft dough. Add remaining water
if necessary.
3 Knead dough briefly on a lightly
floured surface until smooth. Roll out,
using a floured rolling pin, to a
30 cm round.
4 Spread surface with spring onion
mixture then cut dough into twelve
even-sized wedges. Roll each section
from the widest end to form a crescent
shape. Place crescents on prepared
tray 5 cm apart. Brush with milk and
sprinkle with paprika. Bake for 15–20
minutes or until golden brown.
Transfer to a wire rack and cover
with a clean tea towel to keep the
scones soft.

COOK'S FILE

Note: Scones are best eaten on the
day of baking, however they can be
reheated the next day in a 160°C oven.
Scones can also be frozen for up to a
month. Wrap in foil, then place in an
airtight container.

*Cook spring onions until soft, then add
curry powder, parsley and cheese.*

*Roll up each dough triangle to form a
crescent shape.*

SAVOURY CHEESE RING

Preparation time: 30 minutes
Total cooking time: 40 minutes
Makes one ring

1 tablespoon olive oil
3 rashers bacon, finely
   chopped
1 small red onion,
   finely chopped
1/2 red capsicum,
   finely chopped
4 small gherkins, very
   finely chopped
1/2 cup grated cheddar cheese
1/4 cup grated parmesan cheese
1/4 cup fresh parsley, finely
   chopped
1/2 teaspoon dried basil

Dough
21/2 cups self-raising flour
30 g butter, cut into small
   pieces
1/3 cup grated cheddar cheese
1 egg, lightly beaten
3/4 cup milk
sesame seeds, for sprinkling

1 Preheat oven to 180°C. Brush an oven tray with melted butter or oil. Heat oil in a small pan; add bacon, onion and capsicum and cook over low heat 5 minutes or until onion has softened. Drain on paper towels and cool. Combine the cooled bacon mixture, gherkins, cheeses, parsley and basil in a bowl.

2 To make Dough: Sift flour into a large bowl. Add butter and rub in lightly using your fingertips. Add cheese and mix thoroughly. Make a well in the centre. Add egg and almost all the milk. Mix quickly, using a flat-bladed knife, to a soft dough, adding more liquid if necessary.

3 Knead dough briefly on a lightly floured surface. Using a floured rolling pin, roll out to a 30 x 40 cm rectangle. Spread dough evenly with bacon mixture. Roll up from long side and place roll seam-side down on prepared tray. Form into a circle, brush ends with milk and pinch ends together to seal. Using scissors, make deep cuts in sides of dough at 5 cm intervals. Flatten top of ring slightly and brush with milk. Sprinkle with

sesame seeds. Bake for 30–35 minutes or until golden brown.

COOK'S FILE

Storage time: Cheese Ring is best eaten on the day of baking, but can be stored in an airtight container and reheated, covered with foil, in a 180°C oven for 15–20 minutes.

Variation: Ham or salami can be used instead of bacon. Use a chopped zucchini for a vegetarian version.

Mix dough quickly and lightly with a flat-bladed knife.

Using scissors, make small cuts in the dough every 5 cm or so.

PIZZA SCONE

Preparation time: 25 minutes +
1 hour standing
Total cooking time: 30 minutes
Makes one pizza

Tomato Sauce
1 tablespoon water
1/4 cup tomato paste
1–2 cloves crushed garlic
1 teaspoon dried oregano
freshly ground black pepper,
    to taste

2 cups self-raising flour
30 g butter, melted
1/2 cup milk
1/3 cup water
1/2 cup chopped ham, salami or
    pepperoni
1/2 small onion, finely sliced
1/2 cup sliced mushrooms
1/4 red or green capsicum,
    chopped
1/4 cup drained pineapple pieces

12 black olives
1/2 cup grated cheddar or
    mozzarella cheese

1 To make Tomato Sauce:
Combine the water, tomato paste,
garlic, oregano and pepper in a small
bowl. Set aside for one hour to allow
the flavours to combine.
2 Preheat oven to 210°C (190°C gas).
Brush a 28 cm pizza tray with melted
butter or oil. Sift the flour into a large
bowl. Make a well in the centre. Add
combined melted butter, milk and
almost all of the water. Mix quickly,
with a flat-bladed knife, to a soft
dough, adding remaining water
if necessary. Knead the dough briefly
on a lightly floured surface until
smooth. Using a floured rolling pin,
roll dough into a 30 cm circle to fit
pizza tray (or roll into a 35 x 25 cm
rectangle); place on prepared tray.
Crimp outer edge of circle 2 cm to
form a lip.
3 Spread dough with Tomato Sauce,
then sprinkle with chopped ham,

onion, sliced mushrooms, capsicum,
pineapple pieces, olives and cheese.
Bake for 25–30 minutes or until crisp
and golden.

COOK'S FILE

Storage time: Pizza Scone can be
reheated in a 160°C oven for about
20 minutes. Sprinkle with 1/2 cup extra
grated cheese before reheating.
Note: The scone-dough base must be
thoroughly cooked, so do not make
pizza topping too thick.

Crimp the outer edge of the circle to
form a lip; fold lip inside dish.

CHEESE TOPPED SCONES

Preparation time: 15 minutes
Total cooking time: 18 minutes
Makes about 8

2 cups self-raising flour
pinch salt
30 g butter, cut into pieces
1 tablespoon chopped chives
   (optional)
3/4 cup milk

Cheese Topping
30 g butter
1/2 cup grated cheddar cheese
2 teaspoons mustard
ground black pepper, to taste

1 Preheat oven to 210° C (190°C gas). Brush an oven tray with melted butter or oil. Sift the flour and salt into a large bowl. Add the butter; rub in using your fingertips. Stir in chives, if using.

2 Make a well in the centre of the flour mixture. Add almost all of the milk. Quickly mix, using a flat-bladed knife, to a soft dough, adding more liquid if necessary. (The dough should have just lost its stickiness, but not become dried or tough.) Knead dough briefly on a lightly floured surface until smooth. Press or roll out to form a round about 2 cm thick. Cut into scones using a floured 5 cm cutter. Place scones close together on prepared tray. Spoon over Cheese Topping and spread scones slightly. Bake for 10–15 minutes or until golden. Serve warm.

3 To make Cheese Topping: Combine butter, cheese, mustard and pepper in a small pan and stir over low heat until cheese and butter have melted.

COOK'S FILE

Variations: Use your favourite cheese in the Topping, or use a combination of cheeses. You can also add fresh herbs such as chives, basil or parsley to the Topping.

Spoon about one teaspoon of Cheese Topping over each round.

CHEESE AND BACON BUTTERMILK SCONES

Preparation time: 10 minutes
Total cooking time: 25 minutes
Makes about 24

2 teaspoons oil
2 rashers bacon, chopped
4 cups self-raising flour
60 g butter, cut into small
    pieces
1/2 cup grated cheddar cheese
1 tablespoon chopped parsley
    (optional)
1 3/4 cups buttermilk

1 Preheat oven to 210°C (190°C gas). Brush an oven tray with melted butter. Heat oil in pan; cook bacon until crisp. Drain on paper towels. Sift the flour into a large bowl. Add the butter; rub in using your fingertips. Add the cheese, bacon and parsley; stir to combine. Make a well in the centre of the flour mixture. Add almost all of the buttermilk. Quickly mix, using a flat-bladed knife, to a soft dough, adding more buttermilk if necessary.

2 Knead dough briefly on a lightly floured surface until smooth. Press or roll out to form a round about 2 cm thick. Cut into rounds using a floured plain 5 cm cutter. Place scones close together on prepared tray. Brush with any remaining buttermilk. Bake for 15–20 minutes or until golden brown. Serve warm with butter.

Note: Scones freeze well; cool completely on a wire rack. Place in freezer bags or wrap in foil. Seal and label. Freeze until required. Thaw scones completely before reheating.

Add the cooked bacon, cheese and chopped parsley to the flour mixture.

CHEESE HERB SCROLLS

Preparation time: 35 minutes
Total cooking time: 30 minutes
Makes 10

3 cups self-raising flour
pinch baking powder
45 g butter, chopped
2/3 cup milk
1/3 cup water
1 cup grated cheddar cheese
1/2 cup grated parmesan cheese
1/2 cup chopped parsley
1 tablespoon chopped fresh
tarragon
1 tablespoon chopped oregano
1 tablespoon chopped rosemary
15 g butter, extra, softened

1 egg yolk, beaten
2 teaspoons water

1 Preheat oven to 210°C (190°C gas). Brush a 23 cm round cake tin with melted butter or oil; line the base and sides with baking paper. Sift flour and baking powder into a large bowl; rub in butter using your fingertips.
2 Make a well in the centre; add milk and almost all of the water. Mix lightly, using a flat-bladed knife, to a soft dough, adding more water if necessary. Knead briefly on a lightly floured surface until smooth. Roll out to a 40 x 30 cm rectangle.
3 Combine cheeses and herbs in a bowl. Spread softened butter thinly over dough; top with cheese mixture.

4 Roll up dough from one short end. Cut dough crosswise into 10 equal slices. Arrange, cut-side up, in prepared tin. Combine egg yolk and water; brush over slices. Bake 25–30 minutes or until golden brown. Serve warm.

Arrange the scrolls, cut-side up, close together in the prepared tin.

37

MUFFINS

HOW TO MAKE PERFECT MUFFINS

Muffins have everything going for them—they are quick to prepare, quick to cook, great for breakfast, brunch, teatime or snacks... and, of course, they are delicious too.

After reading through the recipe and assembling the ingredients, heat the oven and prepare the tins. (See Note.)

1 Sift the dry ingredients into a large bowl; this helps to make light muffins by aerating the flour and also ensures the dry ingredients are evenly mixed.

2 Put the liquid ingredients in a jug and beat lightly with a fork or whisk. Make a well in the centre of the dry ingredients and pour in the liquid.

3 Stir the mixture gently with a rubber spatula, wooden or metal spoon, or fork until *just* combined; 12 or 15 strokes is usually enough. The mixture will still be a little lumpy but this is what we want. Over-beating will make the cooked muffins tough. (Batter that has had all the lumps beaten out of it will produce pointy tops and large holes inside the cooked product—sure signs of rubbery muffins.)

4 Next, divide the mixture evenly between the muffin tins; use a metal spoon and a smaller spoon to scrape the batter. Try to use the tin size indicated in the recipe; if you use different size tins the cooking time will change. (Smaller muffins will cook more quickly.)

5 Muffins can be tested by inserting a skewer into the centre, as if testing a cake. If the skewer comes out clean the muffin is ready. Alternatively, press the muffin lightly with your fingertip—it is cooked when it feels firm and springs back.

6 Leave the cooked muffins in the tins for a couple of minutes as they will be quite fragile at first. Using a knife, gently loosen muffins from the tin and turn out onto a wire rack to cool. (Muffins can, of course, be eaten while still warm.) Don't leave them in the tins for too long as trapped steam will make the bottoms soggy.

Storage: Cooled muffins can be sealed in an airtight freezer bag and frozen for up to 3 months. Thaw then reheat in a 180°C oven.

Notes: We used the American-style non-stick tins which are available in most supermarkets and department stores. Tins are available in three sizes: mini, regular and large. Unless otherwise indicated, use regular size muffin tins—either the 6- or 12-hole variety.

While all muffin tins have non-stick surfaces, brushing the base of the cup with melted butter or oil is a reasonable precaution, especially when making sweet muffins, because the sugar content can make them sticky.

Sifting the dry ingredients makes for lighter, airier muffins.

Make a well in the centre of the mixture and add liquid ingredients all at once.

Being careful not to beat out the lumps, stir the batter with a wooden spoon.

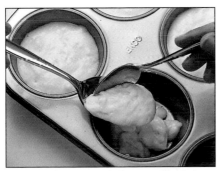
Spoon the batter evenly into muffin holes using two spoons.

Muffins are ready when their tops are golden and they are springy to touch.

Remove muffins from oven and loosen from tin with a flat-bladed knife.

Pumpkin and Prune Muffins, page 49

PLAIN MUFFINS

Preparation time: 15 minutes
Total cooking time: 25 minutes
Makes 12

2¹/2 cups self-raising flour
¹/4 cup caster sugar
2 teaspoons baking powder
2 eggs, lightly beaten
1¹/2 cups milk
160 g butter, melted

1 Preheat oven to moderately hot 210°C (190°C gas). Brush a 12-hole muffin tin with melted butter or oil.
2 Sift flour, sugar and baking powder into a bowl. Make a well in the centre; add combined egg, milk and melted butter all at once.
3 Stir gently with a fork or rubber spatula until mixture is just moistened. (Do not over-mix; batter should look quite lumpy.)
4 Spoon mixture evenly into prepared tin. Bake 20–25 minutes until golden brown. Loosen muffins with a spatula and transfer to a wire rack.

COOK'S FILE

Topping suggestion: Beat ¹/3 cup cream with 1 tablespoon icing sugar until soft peaks form. Cut a circle from the top of each muffin, about 2 cm deep; cut these circles in half to make 'wings'. Spoon ¹/2 teaspoon good quality strawberry jam into each muffin; top with cream mixture and arrange 'wings' in cream.

BANANA MUFFINS

Preparation time: 15 minutes
Total cooking time: 15 minutes
Makes 12

2 cups self-raising flour
1 cup oat bran
3/4 cup caster sugar
60 g butter, melted
3/4 cup milk
2 eggs, lightly beaten
1 cup mashed, ripe banana
    (2 medium bananas)

1 Preheat oven to 210°C (gas 190°C). Brush a 12-hole muffin tin with melted butter or oil. Sift the flour into a large bowl, add the oat bran and the sugar. Make a well in centre of the mixture.

2 Add combined butter, milk, eggs and banana all at once. Using a wooden or metal spoon, stir until just mixed. (Do not over-beat; the batter should remain lumpy.)

3 Spoon mixture into prepared tin. Bake 15 minutes or until puffed and brown. Transfer muffins to a wire rack to cool.

COOK'S FILE

Topping suggestion: For muffins with a difference, beat 100 g cream cheese, 2 tablespoons icing sugar and 2 teaspoons lemon juice with electric beaters until light and creamy. Spread over the muffins and top with dried banana slices.

Make a well in the centre of the mixture and pour in the liquid ingredients.

CRUNCHY TOPPED PEAR MUFFINS

Preparation time: 20 minutes
Total cooking time: 15–20 minutes
Makes 12

2 cups plain flour
1 tablespoon baking
  powder
1/2 teaspoon mixed spice
1/4 cup soft brown sugar
1 firm ripe pear, peeled, cored
  and chopped
1/2 cup raisins
1 egg, lightly beaten
1/3 cup oil
2/3 cup apple juice

Crunchy Topping
1/3 cup walnuts, finely chopped
2 tablespoons soft brown sugar
2 tablespoons plain flour
1/2 teaspoon mixed spice
30 g butter, cubed

1 Preheat oven to 210°C (190°C gas). Brush a 12-hole muffin tin with melted butter or oil.
2 Sift flour, baking powder and spice into a large bowl. Stir in brown sugar. Gently fold through pear and raisins. Make a well in the centre of the flour mixture.
3 Add combined egg, oil and apple juice all at once. Mix quickly with a fork until all ingredients are just moistened. (Do not over-mix; batter should apear quite lumpy.) Spoon mixture evenly into prepared tins. Sprinkle with Crunchy Topping.
4 To make Crunchy Topping: Combine nuts, brown sugar, flour and spice in small bowl. Rub in butter using fingertips.
5 Bake muffins for 15–20 minutes or until golden brown. Loosen muffins with a flat-bladed knife, then turn out onto a wire rack. Dust with sifted icing sugar, if desired.

COOK'S FILE

Storage time: Muffins are best eaten on the day of baking, however freshly baked muffins can be frozen. Seal in airtight freezer bags and store for up to 3 months.

APRICOT MUFFINS

Preparation time: 15 minutes
Total cooking time: 25 minutes
Makes about 12

2 cups plain flour
1 tablespoon baking powder
1/4 teaspoon ground nutmeg
1 cup chopped dried
   apricots
1/2 cup soft brown sugar
1/2 cup chopped pecans

1 teaspoon grated orange
   rind
125 g butter, melted
3/4 cup milk
1 egg, lightly beaten

1 Preheat oven to 210°C (190°C gas). Brush a 12-hole muffin tin with melted butter or oil. Sift the flour, baking powder and nutmeg into a large bowl. Stir in the apricots, sugar, pecans and rind. Make a well in the centre. Add combined butter, milk and egg all at once.

2 Mix lightly until just combined. (Do not over-mix; batter should look quite lumpy.) Spoon mixture into prepared tin. Bake 20–25 minutes or until golden. Loosen muffins with a spatula or flat-bladed knife, then turn onto a wire rack.

COOK'S FILE

Variation: Mix 250 g blueberries or sliced fresh strawberries into the batter in place of apricots. A mashed banana or a cup of canned pie apple can also be used.

DOUBLE CHOC MUFFINS

Preparation time: 15 minutes
Total cooking time: 12–15 minutes
Makes 6 large muffins

2 cups plain flour
2¹/₂ teaspoons baking powder
¹/₄ cup cocoa powder
2 tablespoons caster sugar
1 cup dark choc bits
1 egg, lightly beaten
¹/₂ cup sour cream
³/₄ cup milk
90 g butter, melted

1 Preheat oven to 180°C. Brush a 6-hole large muffin tin with melted butter or oil. Sift flour, baking powder and cocoa into a large bowl. Add sugar and choc bits and mix through. Make a well in the centre of the mixture.

2 Add the combined egg, sour cream, milk and melted butter all at once and stir with a fork until just combined. (Do not over-beat; batter should look quite lumpy.)

3 Spoon the muffin batter evenly into the prepared muffin tin. Bake for 12–15 minutes, or until the muffins are firm. Loosen the muffins with a flat-bladed knife and turn onto a wire rack to cool.

COOK'S FILE

Topping suggestion: Combine 50 g chocolate, 1 tablespoon cream and 10 g butter in a pan; stir over low heat until smooth. Refrigerate mixture until spreadable consistency, then pipe or dollop over muffins. Sprinkle with icing sugar, if desired.

The muffins can be topped with a chocolate and cream mixture.

MUESLI MUFFINS

Preparation time: 15 minutes +
20 minutes standing
Total cooking time: 25 minutes
Makes 6 large muffins

1/2 cup dried apricots,
chopped
1/2 cup orange juice
2 teaspoons finely grated
orange rind
1 cup wholemeal
self-raising flour
1/2 cup self-raising flour
1/2 teaspoon baking powder
1/4 cup soft brown sugar
3/4 cup toasted muesli
1 cup milk
60 g butter, melted

Topping
1 tablespoon plain flour
1/2 teaspoon cinnamon
1/4 cup soft brown sugar
1/3 cup toasted muesli
20 g butter, melted

1 Preheat oven to 210°C (190°C gas). Brush a 6-hole large muffin tin with melted butter or oil. Combine apricots, orange juice and rind in a bowl. Set mixture aside for 20 minutes. (This will slightly soften the apricots.)
2 Sift flours and baking powder into bowl; add sugar and muesli and stir through. Make a well in the centre.
3 Add combined milk, melted butter and undrained apricot mixture all at once. Mix quickly with a fork until all ingredients are just moistened. (Do not over-mix; batter should be lumpy.)
4 Spoon mixture evenly into the prepared tin. Sprinkle with Topping. Bake muffins 20–25 minutes or until golden brown. Loosen muffins with a flat-bladed knife or spatula, then turn onto a wire rack.

To make Topping: Combine flour, cinnamon, sugar, muesli and butter in a bowl; stir to combine.

COOK'S FILE

Storage time: Muffins can be frozen; seal in airtight freezer bags and freeze for up to 3 months. Reheat in a 180°C oven 10 minutes.
Variation: Use other dried fruits, such as dates or figs, if preferred.

Spoon the Topping onto the muffins before baking.

STRAWBERRY AND PASSIONFRUIT MUFFINS

Preparation time: 20 minutes
Total cooking time: 15 minutes
Makes 12

1³/4 cup self-raising flour
pinch salt
1 teaspoon baking powder
¹/2 teaspoon bicarbonate
  of soda
¹/4 cup caster sugar
1 cup chopped fresh
  strawberries

¹/2 cup canned (or fresh)
  passionfruit pulp
1 egg
³/4 cup milk
60 g butter, melted

1 Preheat oven to 210°C (190°C gas). Brush a 12-hole muffin tin with melted butter or oil.
2 Sift flour, salt, baking powder, soda and sugar into bowl. Add strawberries and stir to combine. Make a well in the centre.
3 Add passionfruit pulp and combined egg and milk. Pour melted butter into flour mixture all at once and lightly stir with a fork until just combined. (Do not over-beat; the batter should be quite lumpy.)
4 Spoon mixture into prepared tins and bake 10–15 minutes or until golden brown. Loosen muffins with a flat- bladed knife or spatula and turn out onto a wire rack to cool. Top with whipped cream and fresh strawberry halves and sprinkle with icing sugar, if desired.

COOK'S FILE

Note: Folding the fruit through the dry mixture helps it to be evenly distributed throughout.

COFFEE PECAN STREUSEL MUFFINS

Preparation time: 20 minutes
Total cooking time: 12 minutes
Makes 9

1³/4 cups self-raising flour
1 teaspoon baking powder
1/4 cup caster sugar
1/2 cup finely chopped
   pecans
1 tablespoon instant coffee
   powder
1 tablespoon boiling water
1 egg
3/4 cup milk
1/3 cup oil

Streusel Topping
30 g butter
1/4 cup self-raising flour
2 tablespoons soft brown sugar
1 teaspoon cinnamon
2 tablespoons chopped pecans

1 Preheat oven to 210°C (190°C gas). Brush 9 holes of a 12-hole muffin tin with melted butter or oil. Sift flour and baking powder into a bowl; add caster sugar and pecans. Make a well in the centre.
2 Combine coffee powder with boiling water; stir until dissolved. Cool and add to flour mixture with the combined egg, milk and oil; stir mixture until just combined. (Do not overbeat; batter should look quite lumpy.)
3 Spoon into prepared tin. Sprinkle with Streusel Topping and bake 10–12 minutes until golden brown. Loosen muffins with a flat-bladed knife or spatula and transfer to a wire rack to cool. Sprinkle with icing sugar, if desired.

4 To make Streusel Topping: Rub butter into flour until mixture resembles coarse breadcrumbs. Add sugar, cinnamon and pecans and mix until combined.

COOK'S FILE

Note: For lighter muffins omit the Streusel Topping.

Add sugar, pecans and cinnamon to the Streusel Topping.

ORANGE POPPYSEED MUFFINS

Preparation time: 20 minutes
Total cooking time: 12 minutes
Makes 12

1³/₄ **cups self-raising flour**
1 **tablespoon caster sugar**
1 **teaspoon baking powder**
¹/₄ **teaspoon bicarbonate of soda**
1 **tablespoon poppyseeds**
90 g **butter**
¹/₂ **cup orange marmalade**
1 **egg, lightly beaten**
³/₄ **cup milk**
icing sugar, for sprinkling

1 Preheat oven to 210°C (190°C gas). Brush a 12-hole muffin tin with melted butter or oil. Sift flour, sugar, baking powder and soda into bowl; add poppyseeds and stir. Make a well in the centre.
2 Combine butter and marmalade in small pan; stir over low heat until marmalade becomes runny and butter has melted. Add butter mixture and combined egg and milk to flour mixture; stir until just combined. (Do not over-beat; the batter should be quite lumpy.)
3 Spoon batter into prepared tin and cook 10–12 minutes or until golden. Loosen muffins with a flat-bladed knife or spatula and transfer to a wire rack to cool. Sprinkle with icing sugar.

COOK'S FILE

Topping suggestion: Beat 60 g soft butter, 2 tablespoons icing sugar and 1 teaspoon orange rind together until light and creamy. Cut a small section from the top of the muffin and fill with butter mixture; replace tops.

Make a small hollow in the top of the muffin to accommodate Topping.

PUMPKIN AND PRUNE MUFFINS

Preparation time: 15 minutes
Total cooking time: 20 minutes
Makes 12

1½ cups wholemeal self-raising
    flour
2 teaspoons baking powder
1 teaspoon mixed spice
⅓ cup rolled oats
⅔ cup soft brown sugar
1 cup cooked mashed pumpkin

¾ cup pitted prunes, chopped
1 egg, lightly beaten
125 g butter, melted

1 Preheat oven to 210°C (190°C gas).
Brush a 12-hole muffin tin with
melted butter or oil.
2 Sift flour, baking powder and spice
into a large bowl, returning the husks
to the bowl. Add oats and sugar. Stir
and make a well in the centre.
3 Add combined pumpkin, prunes,
egg and butter all at once. Stir with a
fork or rubber spatula until all ingredients are just combined. (Do not

over-mix; the batter should look
quite lumpy.)
4 Spoon mixture into prepared tin.
Bake for 20 minutes or until golden
brown. Loosen muffins with a flat-
bladed knife or spatula and turn out
onto wire rack to cool.

COOK'S FILE

Note: Muffins derive their characteristic texture from batter containing
slightly unincorporated flour. It
is important, therefore, not to over-
mix the batter or a tough, flat muffin
will result.

BLUEBERRY MUFFINS

Preparation time: 20 minutes
Total cooking time: 20 minutes
Makes 6 large muffins

3 cups plain flour
1 tablespoon baking powder
3/4 cup soft brown sugar
125 g butter, melted
2 eggs, lightly beaten
1 cup milk
1 cup blueberries
icing sugar, for sprinkling

1 Preheat oven to 210°C (190°C gas). Brush a 6-hole large muffin tin with melted butter or oil. Sift the flour and baking powder into a large bowl. Stir in sugar; make a well in the centre.
2 Add combined melted butter, eggs and milk all at once; stir until just blended. (Do not over-mix; the batter should look quite lumpy.)
3 Fold in the blueberries thoroughly, but very lightly. Spoon the batter into prepared tin. Bake for 20 minutes or until golden brown. Loosen muffins with a flat-bladed knife and transfer to a wire rack to cool. Sprinkle with icing sugar.

COOK'S FILE

Note: If fresh blueberries are unavailable, use frozen ones. Thaw and drain very well before using. Other berries can also be used. Try raspberries, blackberries or mulberries, or a combination of these.

Using a metal spoon, fold in berries thoroughly, but very lightly.

BERRY CHEESECAKE MUFFINS

Preparation time: 15 minutes
Total cooking time: 30 minutes
Makes 6 large muffins

1³/4 cups self-raising flour
2 eggs, lightly beaten
1/4 cup oil
2 tablespoons raspberry jam
1/4 cup mixed berry
   yoghurt
1/2 cup caster sugar
50 g cream cheese
1 tablespoon raspberry jam,
   extra, for filling
icing sugar, sifted, for
   dusting

1 Preheat oven to 180°C. Brush a 6-hole muffin tin (large-cup capacity) with melted butter or oil. Sift the flour into a large bowl; make a well in the centre. Add the combined eggs, oil, jam, yoghurt and sugar all at once. Mix the batter until just combined. (Do not over-beat; batter should look quite lumpy.)

2 Spoon three-quarters of the mixture into prepared tin. Cut the cream cheese into 6 equal portions and place a portion on the centre of each muffin. Spread tops with jam; cover with remaining muffin batter.

3 Bake 30 minutes or until muffins are golden brown. Loosen muffins with a flat-bladed knife then turn onto wire rack to cool. Dust muffins with icing sugar to serve.

COOK'S FILE

Note: These muffins are best eaten as soon as they are cool enough. The cream cheese filling will melt slightly as the muffins cook and provide a delicious 'surprise' centre.

Place a portion of cream cheese on the centre of each muffin.

CHOC-SULTANA MUFFINS

Preparation time: 10 minutes
Total cooking time: 20–25 minutes
Makes about 12

2 cups self-raising flour
1/4 cup soft brown sugar
1/2 cup sultanas
1/4 cup choc bits
1/2 cup sour cream
2 eggs, lightly beaten
90 g butter, melted
1/4 cup milk

1 Preheat oven to 180°C. Brush a 12-hole muffin tin with melted butter or oil. Sift flour into a large bowl. Add sugar, sultanas and choc bits; stir. Make a well in centre of the mixture.
2 Add combined sour cream, eggs, butter and milk all at once.
3 Mix lightly until just combined. (Do not over-mix; batter should look quite lumpy.) Spoon mixture into prepared tin. Bake 20–25 minutes or until golden. Loosen muffins with a flat-bladed knife or spatula, then turn onto a wire rack to cool. Dust with sifted icing sugar, if desired.

COOK'S FILE

Variations: Add extra choc bits for added crunch, or use a combination of dark, milk and white chocolate pieces. Choc dots, which are smaller than choc bits, can also be used if a less lumpy texture is preferred. The chocolate will melt slightly during cooking.
Note: Muffin tins are available from supermarkets. Choose the non-stick variety, with either six or twelve cups. Mini muffin tins or large-cup muffin tins are available from speciality kitchen shops.

WHITE CHOCOLATE MANGO MUFFINS

Preparation time: 10 minutes
Total cooking time: 20 minutes
Makes 12

2½ cups self-raising flour
½ cup soft brown sugar
¾ cup white choc bits
1 cup chopped fresh mango flesh (2 medium) or 440 g can mango pieces, well drained

½ cup milk
¼ cup cream
90 g butter, melted
1 egg, lightly beaten

1 Preheat oven to 180°C. Brush a 12-hole muffin tin with melted butter or oil. Sift the flour into a large bowl. Stir in the sugar and choc bits and mix well. Fold in chopped mango gently. Make a well in the centre of the mixture.
2 Add the combined milk, cream, butter and egg all at once. Mix with a fork or rubber spatula until just combined. (Do not over-mix; batter should look quite lumpy.) Spoon the mixture into prepared tin.
3 Bake for 20 minutes or until golden. Loosen muffins with a flat-bladed knife and turn onto a wire rack to cool.

COOK'S FILE

Note: These muffins can be served warm, with whipped cream. They make an unusual, but delicious, dessert, topped with large shavings of white chocolate or served split with stewed apples or apricots.
Variation: Use dark or milk choc bits in these muffins if you prefer.

BANANA CRUMBLE MUFFINS

Preparation time: 15 minutes
Total cooking time: 20 minutes
Makes 12

2 cups wholemeal self-raising
    flour
1/3 cup raw sugar
1/2 teaspoon nutmeg
1 cup mashed bananas
    (2–3 medium bananas)
1 egg, lightly beaten
1/4 cup oil
1/2 cup yoghurt

Crumble Topping
25 g butter
1/4 cup plain flour,
    sifted
1 tablespoon soft brown sugar

1 tablespoon sunflower seeds
    (or pumpkin seeds)

1 Preheat oven to 210°C (190°C gas). Brush a 12-hole muffin tin with melted butter or oil.
2 Sift flour into a large bowl, returning the husks to the bowl. Stir in sugar and nutmeg. Make a well in the centre of the mixture.
3 Add the combined banana, egg, oil and yoghurt all at once; mix with a fork or rubber spatula until just combined. (Do not over-beat; batter should be quite lumpy.) Spoon the mixture into prepared tin. Sprinkle with Crumble Topping. Bake for 20 minutes or until golden. Loosen muffins with a flat-bladed knife or spatula and transfer to a wire rack to cool.
4 To make Crumble Topping: Rub butter into flour until well combined. Stir in brown sugar and seeds.

COOK'S FILE

Note: Allow muffins to slightly cool in their tins for a minute or so before turning out onto a wire rack to cool. If muffins are left to cool completely in tins the trapped-steam will make the bottoms go soggy.
Variation: Use white self-raising flour, if you prefer.

Sprinkle the uncooked muffins with Crumble Topping.

54

PUMPKIN AND POPPYSEED MUFFINS

Preparation time: 20 minutes
Total cooking time: 25 minutes
Makes 6 large muffins

1 cup plain flour
1 cup wholemeal plain
    flour
1 tablespoon baking powder
1 teaspoon nutmeg
2 tablespoons poppyseeds
1/3 cup soft brown sugar
60 g butter, melted
1 cup cooked pumpkin, cooled
    and mashed
1 egg, lightly beaten
1 cup milk

1 Preheat oven to 210°C (190°C gas). Brush a 6 hole muffin tin (large-cup capacity) with melted butter or oil. Sift flours, baking powder and nutmeg into a large bowl, returning flour husks to bowl. Stir in poppyseeds and sugar and mix well. Make a well in the centre.
2 Add combined butter, pumpkin, egg and milk all at once. Mix quickly with a fork until all ingredients are just moistened. (Do not over-mix; batter should look quite lumpy.)
3 Spoon batter evenly into tins. Bake for 20–25 minutes or until golden brown. Remove from oven and leave in tin 5 minutes, then turn out onto a wire rack to cool.

COOK'S FILE

Note: 500 g uncooked pumpkin will produce one cup of mashed pumpkin. Peel, cube and cook pumpkin in microwave or over heat until tender; drain well then mash and cool.

Add sugar and poppyseeds to the sifted flours and mix well.

FRUITY BRAN MUFFINS

Preparation time: 15 minutes +
 20 minutes standing
Total cooking time: 20 minutes
Makes 12

2 cups unprocessed bran
1½ cups milk
¼ cup soft brown sugar
¼ cup golden syrup
2 eggs, lightly beaten
1½ cups plain flour
1 tablespoon baking
 powder
1 cup chopped dried fruit
 medley

1 Preheat oven to 210°C (190°C gas). Brush a 12-hole muffin tin with melted butter or oil. Combine bran and milk in a bowl. Add sugar, golden syrup and eggs. Stir to combine and leave bran to soften for 20 minutes.
2 Sift flour and baking powder into a large bowl. Add fruit medley and mix thoroughly. Make a well in the centre.
3 Add bran mixture all at once. Mix until all ingredients are just combined. (Do not over-mix.)
4 Spoon mixture into prepared tin. Bake for 20 minutes or until golden. Loosen muffins with a flat-bladed knife or spatula, then turn out onto wire rack to cool.

COOK'S FILE

Storage time: Muffins are best eaten on the day of baking but can be frozen, sealed in airtight freezer bags, for up to 3 months.
Variation: Use other dried fruit such as dates or prunes, if preferred.

FRUIT AND NUT MUFFINS

Preparation time: 15 minutes
Total cooking time: 20 minutes
Makes 12

2 cups self-raising flour
1 teaspoon ground mixed spice
1 cup chopped dried fruit
 medley
½ cup chopped mixed nuts
125 g butter
½ cup caster sugar
2 eggs, lightly beaten
¾ cup milk

1 Preheat oven to 210°C (190°C gas). Brush a 12-hole muffin tin with melted butter or oil. Sift flour and spice into large bowl. Add the fruit

medley and mixed nuts; stir until combined. Make a well in the centre of the mixture.

2 Melt butter and sugar in a small pan over low heat, stirring until the sugar has dissolved; remove from heat. Combine eggs and milk in a small bowl.

3 Add the butter and egg mixtures all at once to the flour mixture. Using a metal spoon or fork, stir until all the ingredients are just combined. (Do not over-beat; the batter should look lumpy.)

4 Spoon mixture into prepared tin. Bake 20 minutes or until golden. Loosen muffins with a flat-bladed knife, then turn onto wire rack to cool.

Left to right: Fruity Bran Muffins, Fig and Oat Bran Muffins and Fruit and Nut Muffins

FIG AND OAT BRAN MUFFINS

Preparation time: 20 minutes
Total cooking time: 20 minutes
Makes 12

1½ cups plain flour
1 tablespoon baking powder
1 teaspoon cinnamon
1 cup oat bran
¼ cup soft brown sugar
1 cup chopped dried figs
1 egg
¾ cup milk
2 tablespoons oil
¼ cup golden syrup

1 Preheat oven to 210°C (190°C gas). Brush a 12-hole muffin tin with melted butter or oil. Sift flour, baking powder and cinnamon into a large bowl. Add the oat bran and sugar and stir thoroughly until all ingredients are well mixed. Stir in the chopped figs. Make a well in the centre of the mixture.

2 Add combined egg, milk, oil and golden syrup all at once. Mix quickly with a fork until all ingredients are just moistened. (Do not over-mix.)

3 Spoon mixture into prepared tin. Bake for 20 minutes or until golden. Remove from oven and leave in tin 5 minutes then turn out onto a wire rack to cool.

COOK'S FILE

Storage time: Muffins are best eaten on the day of baking but can be frozen, sealed in airtight freezer bags, for up to 3 months.
Variation: Other dried fruits, such as apricots, dates, raisins and sultanas are suitable for this recipe. Add half a cup of chopped pecans or hazelnuts to the muffin batter, if you like.

CORNMEAL MUFFINS

Preparation time: 15 minutes
Total cooking time: 10 minutes
Makes 24 mini muffins

1¹/2 cups plain flour
1 cup cornmeal
¹/2 teaspoon salt
1 tablespoon baking powder
¹/4 cup sugar
2 eggs, lightly beaten
¹/4 cup oil
1 cup creamed corn
¹/3 cup finely grated cheese
1 tablespoon chopped parsley
³/4 cup milk

1 Preheat oven to 210°C (190°C gas). Brush two 12-hole mini muffin tins with oil or melted butter. Sift flour, cornmeal, salt, baking powder and sugar into a large bowl. Lightly combine eggs, oil, creamed corn, cheese, parsley and milk in a separate bowl.

2 Make a well in the centre of the cornmeal mixture and add egg mixture all at once. Mix quickly with a fork until all ingredients are just combined. (Do not over-mix; batter should be quite lumpy.)

3 Spoon batter into prepared tins. Bake 10 minutes or until golden. Loosen muffins with a flat-bladed knife or spatula and transfer to a wire rack to cool.

COOK'S FILE

Note: Cornmeal, made from ground corn kernels, is also known as polenta and used in cornbread and muffins.

Using a whisk, combine eggs, oil, corn, cheese, parsley and milk.

SPICY VEGETABLE MUFFINS

Preparation time: 15 minutes
Total cooking time: 25 minutes
Makes 12

2 cups self-raising flour
3 teaspoons curry powder
salt and freshly ground black
    pepper, to taste
1/2 cup grated carrot
1/2 cup grated orange
    sweet potato
1 cup grated cheddar
    cheese
90 g butter, melted

1 egg, lightly beaten
3/4 cup milk

1 Preheat oven to 180°C. Brush a 12-hole muffin tin with oil or melted butter. Sift flour, curry powder, salt and pepper into a bowl. Add carrot, sweet potato and cheese; mix through with your fingertips until evenly combined. Make a well in the centre.
2 Add combined butter, egg and milk all at once. Using a wooden spoon, stir until ingredients are just combined. (Do not over-mix; batter should be quite lumpy.)
3 Spoon mixture into prepared tin. Bake 25 minutes or until puffed and golden. Serve with butter, if desired.

COOK'S FILE

Storage time: Cook this dish just before serving. These muffins are best eaten while still warm.

Mix the dry ingredients, cheese and vegetables using your fingertips.

59

ENGLISH MUFFINS

Preparation time: 20 minutes
  + 1 hour 40 minutes standing
Total cooking time: 15 minutes
Makes 15

7 g sachet dried yeast
1/2 teaspoon sugar
1 teaspoon plain flour
1/4 cup warm water
1 teaspoon salt
4 1/4 cups plain flour, extra
1 1/3 cups lukewarm milk

1 egg, lightly beaten
40 g butter, melted

1 Lightly dust two 32 x 28 cm oven trays with flour. Combine yeast, sugar, flour and water in small bowl; blend until smooth. Stand mixture, covered with plastic wrap, in a warm place for 10 minutes or until foamy. Sift salt and extra flour into a large bowl. Make a well in centre; add milk, egg, butter and yeast mixture all at once. Using a flat-bladed knife, mix to a soft dough.
2 Turn dough onto a lightly floured surface; knead lightly for 2 minutes or until smooth. Shape the dough into a ball; place in large, lightly oiled bowl. Leave, covered with plastic wrap, in a warm place for 1 1/2 hours or until well risen.
3 Preheat oven to 210°C (190°C gas). Knead dough again for 2 minutes or until smooth. Roll dough to 1 cm thickness. Cut into rounds with a plain 8 cm cutter. Place rounds on prepared trays. Leave, covered with plastic wrap, in warm place 10 minutes. Bake for 15 minutes, turning muffins once after 7 or 8 minutes. Cool on a wire rack.

Set aside the yeast mixture until it becomes foamy.

Put the dough ball in a lightly oiled bowl and set it aside to rise.

Cut out muffin rounds with a plain 8 cm cutter.

ZUCCHINI AND CARROT MUFFINS

Preparation time: 20 minutes
Total cooking time: 20 minutes
Makes 12

2 medium zucchini
2 carrots, peeled
2 cups self-raising flour
pinch salt
1 teaspoon cinnamon
1/2 teaspoon nutmeg
1/2 cup chopped pecans
2 eggs
1 cup milk
80 g butter, melted

1 Preheat oven to 210°C (190°C gas). Brush a 12-hole muffin tin with melted butter or oil. Grate zucchini and carrots. Sift flour, salt and cinnamon and nutmeg into a large bowl. Add the carrot, zucchini and chopped pecans. Stir thoroughly until all the ingredients are well combined.

2 Combine the eggs, milk and melted butter in a separate bowl and whisk well until combined.

3 Make a well in the centre of the flour mixture; add the egg mixture all at once. Mix quickly with a fork or rubber spatula until all the ingredients are just moistened. (Do not over-mix; the batter should be quite lumpy.)

4 Spoon batter evenly into prepared tin. Bake 15–20 minutes or until golden. Loosen muffins with a flat-bladed knife or spatula then turn onto a wire rack to cool.

COOK'S FILE

Storage time: Muffins are best eaten on the day of baking, however they can be frozen for up to 3 months. Place them in an airtight container (wrap individually in foil if they are likely to be wanted one at a time). Reheat muffins in a 180°C oven for 10 minutes. There is no need to thaw them before reheating.

Variation: Use well chopped walnuts instead of the pecans, if preferred. Use skim, whole milk or buttermilk in the batter.

Grate zucchini and carrot to produce one cup of each.

61

MINI CHILLI AND CHEESE MUFFINS

Preparation time: 25 minutes
Total cooking time: 8–10 minutes
Makes 24 mini muffins

1 1/2 cups self-raising flour
1 teaspoon baking powder
pinch salt
1 tablespoon caster sugar
1/2 cup cornmeal
1/4 cup grated cheddar
    cheese
1 tablespoon chopped fresh
    coriander leaves
60 g butter
1 small onion, diced
2 chillies, finely chopped
125 g cream cheese, at room
    temperature

1 egg
3/4 cup milk

1 Preheat oven to 210°C (190°C gas). Brush two 12-hole mini muffin tins with oil or melted butter. Sift flour, baking powder and salt into a bowl. Add sugar, cornmeal, cheese and coriander and stir to combine.
2 Melt butter in a small pan and cook onion and chilli until the onion is translucent. Cool slightly then stir into flour mixture. Beat cream cheese and egg in a separate bowl until creamy. Add milk and stir mixture until well combined.
3 Stir milk mixture into flour mixture all at once; stir until just combined. (Do not over-mix; batter should be quite lumpy.) Spoon batter into prepared tins and bake for 8–10 minutes or until golden.

COOK'S FILE

Serving suggestions: Serve this muffin as an accompaniment to soups and stews.
• As an alternative to dumplings, spoon tablespoons of the raw batter on top of a casserole during the last 10 minutes of cooking.

Add the milk mixture all at once to the flour mixture.

PIZZA MUFFINS

Preparation time: 25 minutes
Total cooking time: 15 minutes
Makes 24

1³/4 cups self-raising flour
pinch salt
1 teaspoon baking powder
2 teaspoons caster sugar
1/2 teaspoon garlic salt
1 tablespoon chopped black
    olives, optional
1/3 cup grated cheddar
    cheese
60 g butter
1 small onion, chopped
2 rashers bacon, finely
    chopped
1/2 small green capsicum,
    chopped

1 egg, lightly beaten
1/4 cup tomato paste
3/4 cup milk

1 Preheat the oven to 210°C (190°C gas). Lightly brush two 12-hole muffin tins with oil or melted butter.
2 Sift the flour, salt and baking powder into a bowl. Add the sugar, garlic salt, olives and cheese and stir until they are combined.
3 Melt the butter and cook the onion, bacon and capsicum for 2–3 minutes or until the capsicum starts to soften. Cool slightly, then add to the flour mixture and stir.
4 Combine the egg, tomato paste and milk in a small bowl. Quickly and lightly fold into the flour mixture. (Do not over-mix; muffin batter is better if it is quite lumpy.) Spoon the batter into the tins and bake for about

8–10 minutes or until golden. Loosen the muffins with a flat-bladed knife or spatula and transfer them to a wire rack to cool.

COOK'S FILE

Serving suggestion: Serve pizza muffins warm with a green salad.

Fry the onion, bacon and capsicum until the capsicum begins to soften.

CAPSICUM AND CORN MUFFINS

Preparation time: 15 minutes
Total cooking time: 20 minutes
Makes 12

1 cup plain flour
1/4 teaspoon salt
1 tablespoon baking powder
1 cup fine cornmeal
1 tablespoon caster sugar
1 egg
2/3 cup milk
1/4 teaspoon Tabasco sauce
   (optional)
1/4 cup oil
1/2 red capsicum, finely
   chopped
440 g can corn kernels, drained
1/4 cup parsley, finely chopped

1 Preheat oven to 210°C (190°C gas). Brush a 12-hole muffin tin with oil or melted butter. Sift flour, salt and baking powder into a large bowl. Add the cornmeal and sugar. Stir thoroughly until all the ingredients are well mixed. Make a well in the centre of the mixture.

2 Combine the egg, milk, Tabasco (if using) and oil in a separate bowl. Add the egg mixture, capsicum, corn and parsley all at once to dry ingredients. Stir quickly with a wooden spoon or rubber spatula until all ingredients are just moistened. (Do not over-mix; the batter should be quite lumpy.)

3 Spoon the batter evenly into the prepared tin. Bake for 20 minutes or until golden brown. Remove muffins from oven and leave in tin for 5 minutes, then turn out onto a wire rack to cool.

COOK'S FILE

Storage time: Muffins are best eaten on the day of baking, however they can be frozen for up to 3 months in an airtight container. Wrap them individually in foil if they are going to be needed one at a time. Reheat in moderate oven for 10 minutes.

Stir in egg mixture, capsicum, corn and parsley until just moistened.

SPINACH AND CHEESE MUFFINS

Preparation time: 15 minutes
Total cooking time: 20 minutes
Makes 12

250 g packet frozen chopped
   spinach, thawed
2 cups self-raising flour
1/2 teaspoon ground nutmeg
1 cup finely grated cheddar
   cheese
60 g feta cheese, crumbled
1 cup milk
1 egg
1 tablespoon sesame seeds

1 Preheat oven to 210°C (190°C gas).
Brush a 12 hole muffin tin with oil or
melted butter. Squeeze excess moisture from spinach through a sieve. Sift
flour and nutmeg into a bowl; add
cheeses and stir to combine.
2 Make a well in the centre of
the flour mixture. Add the combined
milk and egg all at once, then add
the spinach.
3 Mix dough lightly until ingredients
are just combined. (Do not over-mix;
batter should be quite lumpy.) Spoon
mixture into prepared tin. Sprinkle
with sesame seeds. Bake for 20
minutes or until golden. Transfer to a
wire rack to cool.

COOK'S FILE

Variations: Fresh spinach can be
used in place of frozen. Remove
stalks, wash leaves and chop finely.
Boil, steam or microwave briefly until
just wilted. Cool and squeeze out
excess moisture. Cooked finely
chopped broccoli can also be used
instead of spinach.

*Use a sieve to squeeze the excess
moisture from the spinach.*

CARAMELISED ONION MUFFINS

Preparation time: 30 minutes
Total cooking time: 20 minutes
Makes 12

2 tablespoons oil
2 large onions, chopped
¼ cup sugar
2¼ cups self-raising
    flour
60 g butter, chopped
1 egg
1 cup milk

1 Preheat oven to 210°C (190°C gas). Brush a 12-hole muffin tin with oil or melted butter. Heat oil in pan; cook onions and sugar, over medium heat, until onion becomes golden in colour and the sugar has dissolved. Allow the mixture to cool.
2 Sift the flour into a large bowl. Rub the butter into the flour until the mixture resembles fine breadcrumbs. Stir in the onion mixture and mix until all the onion is coated in the flour mixture.
3 Beat egg and milk together. Gently fold into onion mixture all at once. (Do not over-beat.) Spoon into prepared

muffin pans. Bake 20 minutes or until golden. Transfer to a wire rack to cool.

Fry onions until they turn golden and the sugar has dissolved.

CORN AND HAM MUFFINS

Preparation time: 10 minutes
Total cooking time: 25 minutes
Makes 12

2 cups self-raising flour
1/4 teaspoon cayenne pepper
1/2 cup chopped ham
130 g can corn niblets,
   drained
1/2 red capsicum, seeded and
   finely chopped
1 tablespoon chopped parsley

125 g butter, melted
1 cup milk
1 egg
2–3 drops Tabasco sauce
1 tablespoon sesame
   seeds

1 Preheat oven to 210°C (190°C gas). Brush a 12-hole muffin tin with oil or melted butter. Sift the flour and cayenne pepper into a large bowl. Add ham, corn, capsicum and parsley; stir to combine.
2 Make a well in the centre of the flour mixture; add combined butter, milk, egg and Tabasco all at once.

Mix dough lightly with a fork or rubber spatula until ingredients are just combined. (Do not over-mix; the batter should be quite lumpy.)
3 Spoon mixture into prepared tin. Sprinkle muffins with sesame seeds. Bake for 20–25 minutes or until golden. Cool on a wire rack.

COOK'S FILE

Variations: If you prefer, use wholemeal flour instead of white. A little extra milk may be required as wholemeal flour absorbs more liquid.
• Use margarine in place of the butter, if you prefer.

67

Add the combined juice, egg, melted butter and almost all of the water.

To test for elasticity, press your finger into dough; it should spring straight back.

Set dough aside to rise in a warm place for about 45 minutes.

TEATIME TREATS

ICED TEA BUN

Preparation time: 30 minutes +
1 hour 10 minutes standing
Total cooking time: 25 minutes
Makes one bun

2 cups plain flour
7 g sachet dried yeast
2 tablespoons caster sugar
2 teaspoons grated orange rind
1/2 cup sultanas
1/3 cup orange juice
1 egg, lightly beaten
30 g butter, melted
1/3 cup warm water

Glacé Icing
1 cup icing sugar
15 g butter
1 tablespoon boiling water
pink food colouring
desiccated coconut, to sprinkle

1 Brush a baking tray with melted butter or oil. Sift flour into a large bowl; add yeast, sugar, rind and sultanas. Stir to combine and make a well in the centre. Add the combined orange juice, beaten egg and melted butter and almost all the water.

2 Mix to a soft dough, adding more water if necessary. Turn out onto a lightly floured surface; knead for 10 minutes, until smooth and elastic. (To test, press the dough: it should spring back without leaving an indent.)

3 Place dough in a large, lightly oiled bowl. Cover with lightly oiled plastic wrap and leave in a warm place for 45 minutes or until well risen. Punch down dough and knead for 1 minute.

4 Shape dough into a smooth ball and roll or pat out to a 25 cm circle. Place on the tray, cover and leave in a warm place to rise for 30 minutes.

5 Preheat oven to 180°C. Mark the dough into 8 wedges with the edge of a ruler. Cook for 20 minutes or until golden brown and cooked through (Dough will sound hollow when tapped.) Turn out onto a wire rack. When cold, spread Glacé Icing over the bun and sprinkle with coconut.

6 **To make Glacé Icing:** Sift icing sugar into a small heatproof bowl. Combine butter and water in a small pan. Stir over low heat until butter has melted; add to sugar. Mix to a smooth paste Stand bowl over pan of simmering water; stir until icing is glossy. Remove from heat. Tint icing with food colouring, as desired.

Roll or pat dough out to a large circle, then set aside to rise again.

Mark the dough into 8 wedges with the edge of a ruler just before baking.

Stir the Glacé Icing over simmering water until it becomes glossy.

CREAM BUNS

Preparation time: 30 minutes +
1 hour 15 minutes standing
Total cooking time: 20 minutes
Makes 12

3¹/₂ cups plain flour
2 tablespoons sugar
pinch salt
1¹/₃ cups milk, warmed
60 g butter, melted
7 g sachet dried yeast
¹/₂ cup raspberry jam
1¹/₄ cups cream
3 tablespoons icing sugar

1 Line a large oven tray with paper; grease paper. Combine flour, sugar and salt in food processor. Combine the milk and butter in a small bowl. Sprinkle the yeast over the milk mixture, stir to dissolve. Pour yeast mixture into the food processor. Process for 30 seconds or until a soft dough forms. Transfer dough to a lightly oiled bowl. Leave, covered with plastic wrap, in warm place 1 hour or until well risen.

2 Turn dough onto a lightly floured surface; knead for about 2 minutes or until smooth. Divide dough into 12 portions. Knead one portion at a time on lightly floured surface for 30 seconds; shape into balls. Preheat oven to 210°C (190°C gas). Place balls of dough evenly apart on prepared tray. Leave, covered with plastic wrap, in warm place 15 minutes or until well risen. Bake buns for 20 minutes or until well browned and cooked through. Stand buns for 5 minutes before transferring to a wire rack to cool.

3 Using a serrated knife, cut about

halfway into the side of each bun. Spread a layer of jam in each crevice. Using electric beaters, beat cream and 1 tablespoon of the icing sugar until firm peaks form. Spoon or pipe over

jam. Dust buns with remaining icing sugar before serving.

COOK'S FILE

Note: Best filled close to serving time.

Process the mixture for about 30 seconds or until a soft dough forms.

Knead dough portions on a lightly floured surface, then shape into balls.

Make a large cut in side of each bun; spread a layer of jam into the crevice.

KRENDL

Preparation time: 40 minutes + 1 hour
30 minutes standing
Total cooking time: 45 minutes
Makes one loaf

7 g sachet dried yeast
2 tablespoons warm water
3/4 cup milk
50 g butter
1/4 cup caster sugar
1 teaspoon vanilla essence
2 egg yolks
1/2 teaspoon salt
3–31/2 cups plain flour
40 g butter, melted
410 g can pie apples
1/2 cup chopped prunes
1/2 cup chopped apricots
1 teaspoon cinnamon

Icing
1 cup icing sugar
1/2 teaspoon vanilla essence
1–2 tablespoons milk
1/2 cup flaked almonds, toasted

1 Brush a large oven tray with oil or melted butter. Dissolve yeast in warm water. Set aside 5 minutes or until frothy. Combine milk, butter and 1 tablespoon of the sugar in a small pan; stir over low heat until butter melts. Remove from heat. Stir in vanilla and egg yolks. Sift salt and 3 cups of the flour into a large bowl; make a well in the centre. Add milk mixture and yeast; stir until well combined. Add enough of the remaining flour to form a soft dough. Turn out onto a lightly floured surface and knead 10 minutes until dough is smooth and elastic. Place dough in a lightly oiled bowl and brush surface of dough with oil. Cover and leave in a warm place 1 hour or until well risen. Knead dough again 1 minute. Roll into a 20 x 75 cm rectangle. Spread with melted butter, apple, prunes and apricots and sprinkle with cinnamon and the remaining sugar.

2 Roll up dough from the longer side and pinch seams and ends to seal. Form into a pretzel shape and place on prepared tray. Tuck ends under dough and flatten slightly. Preheat oven to 180°C. Cover dough and leave to rise in a warm place for 30 minutes or until well risen. Bake for 45–50 minutes or until golden.

3 To make Icing: Combine icing sugar, essence and milk in a small bowl. Spread over Krendl while still warm and sprinkle with almonds. Allow to cool before serving.

Add the milk mixture and the yeast to the flour; stir until well combined.

Roll dough into a large rectangle and spread with butter and fruit.

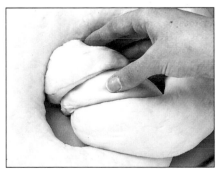

Roll up dough from the longer side and form into a pretzel shape.

FRUIT SCROLLS

Preparation time: 20 minutes +
1 hour 20 minutes standing
Total cooking time: 20 minutes
Makes 20

7 g sachet dried yeast
1 teaspoon sugar
1 tablespoon plain flour
1/2 cup milk, warmed
2 1/2 cups plain flour, extra,
  sifted
185 g butter, chopped
1 tablespoon caster sugar
1 teaspoon mixed spice
1 egg, lightly beaten
2 teaspoons grated lemon
  rind
1/4 cup soft brown sugar
1 1/3 cups mixed dried fruit

Glaze
1 tablespoon milk
2 tablespoons sugar

1 Brush an oven tray with oil or melted butter; line with baking paper. Combine yeast, sugar and flour in a small bowl. Gradually add the milk; blend mixture until smooth. Stand the mixture, covered with plastic wrap, in a warm place for 10 minutes or until foamy.
2 Combine extra flour, 125 g of the butter, caster sugar and 1/2 teaspoon of the spice in food processor. Process for 30 seconds or until mixture is fine and crumbly. Add egg, rind and yeast mixture; process 15 seconds or until mixture just comes together.
3 Turn the mixture onto a lightly floured surface; knead for about 2 minutes or until dough is smooth; shape dough into a ball. Place dough

ball in a lightly oiled bowl. Leave, covered with plastic wrap, in a warm place for 1 hour or until well risen. Knead dough again for 2 minutes or until smooth.
4 Preheat oven to 210°C (gas 190°C). Using electric beaters, beat remaining butter and the brown sugar in a bowl until light and creamy. Roll dough out to a 40 x 35 cm rectangle. Spread the butter mixture over the dough, leaving a 2 cm border along the top. Spread dough with combined fruit and remaining spice. Roll dough firmly and evenly into a log. Using a sharp knife, cut roll into 2 cm thick slices.
5 Arrange slices evenly apart on the prepared tray. Leave, covered with plastic wrap, in warm place for 10 minutes or until well risen. Bake scrolls for 20 minutes or until well browned and cooked through.
6 To make Glaze: Combine milk and sugar in pan. Stir over low heat until sugar dissolves and mixture has almost come to the boil. Remove from heat and brush liberally over scrolls while they are still hot. Place scrolls on a wire rack to cool.

COOK'S FILE

Storage time: Fruit Scrolls can be stored in the freezer for up to 2 months. They will keep in an air-tight container for several days.
Note: This recipe is an adaptation of traditional Chelsea Buns. To make Chelsea Buns prepare the above recipe up to Step 5. Place slices close together (so that their sides are touching) when setting aside to rise. (This will force them to rise and form the characteristic square shape.) Bake as above. Break into individual buns as soon as they cool.

Stand the mixture for 10 minutes or until it becomes foamy.

Process flour, butter, sugar and spices until the mixture is fine and crumbly.

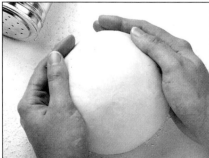

Shape the dough into a ball on a lightly floured surface.

Sprinkle dough with combined chopped fruit and spice.

Arrange Scrolls, spaced well apart, on the prepared tray.

Brush Scrolls with the Glaze while they are still warm.

73

Using electric beaters, beat the mixture for 2 minutes or until smooth.

Cover the dough with lightly oiled plastic wrap; set aside 1 hour.

Shape the dough into 35 cm ropes and form into a braid.

Make a second, smaller braid, then braid remaining dough.

Make a depression in the largest braid and place the second on top.

Brush the loaf with egg white and sprinkle with almonds and sugar.

VIENNESE STRIEZEL

Preparation time: 40 minutes +
  2 hours standing
Total cooking time: 40 minutes
Makes one loaf

2 x 7 g sachets dried yeast
1/4 cup warm water
1/4 cup caster sugar
3/4 cup milk, warmed
1 egg
2 egg yolks
80 g butter, melted
1/2 teaspoon salt
2 teaspoons grated
  lemon rind

4–4 1/2 cups plain flour
1 cup raisins
1 egg white, lightly beaten,
  to glaze
2 tablespoons slivered almonds
caster sugar, extra,
  for sprinkling

1 Combine yeast, warm water and 1 teaspoon of the sugar in large bowl. Leave to stand for 5 minutes or until frothy. Add the milk, egg and egg yolks, butter, remaining sugar, salt, rind and 2 cups of the flour. Using electric beaters, beat 2 minutes or until well combined. Stir in the raisins and enough of the remaining flour to make a soft dough.

2 Turn out dough onto a lightly floured surface. Knead dough for 10 minutes or until smooth and elastic. Place dough in an oiled bowl, cover with lightly oiled plastic wrap and leave in a warm place 1 hour or until well risen. Punch down dough. Knead again 1 minute.

3 Divide dough in half. Cover one portion with a tea towel and set aside. Divide remaining dough into 3 equal pieces. Shape into 35 cm ropes. Place

3 ropes side by side and braid, beginning with the middle braid. Pinch ends to seal and tuck under.

4 Cut off one third of the reserved dough and divide this into 3 equal pieces; shape each piece of dough into 20 cm ropes. Braid the dough and set it aside. Divide the remaining dough into 3 equal pieces and shape each piece into 30 cm ropes. Braid dough and set aside.

5 With the side of your hand, make a 2 cm depression down the middle of the large braid. Brush the braid with egg white. Place the 30 cm braid on top of the first. Make a 2 cm depression down centre of the second braid, brush with egg white and place the smallest braid on top; press down lightly. Brush a baking tray lightly with oil; lift Striezel carefully onto prepared tray.

6 Cover loosely with lightly oiled plastic wrap and leave to rise in warm place for 1 hour or until well risen. Preheat oven to 180°C. Brush loaf with remaining egg white, sprinkle with almonds and the extra caster sugar. Bake 30–40 minutes or until cooked. (Test by tapping base of bread, it will sound hollow when cooked.) Cool on a wire rack.

COOK'S FILE

Storage time: Store for up to 3 days in an airtight container.

STREUSEL KUCHEN

Preparation time: 40 minutes +
2 hours standing
Total cooking time: 55 minutes
Serves 6–8

7 g sachet dried yeast
2 tablespoons lukewarm
    water
1/2 cup milk
1/4 cup caster sugar
50 g butter
1/2 teaspoon salt
2 3/4 cups plain flour
1 egg, lightly beaten
1/2 cup apricot jam
2 tablespoons water or
    lemon juice
2 x 410 g cans pie apple

Crumble Topping
1/2 cup soft brown sugar
1/3 cup plain flour
1 teaspoon cinnamon
60 g butter, cubed
1 cup walnuts, roughly
    chopped

1 Grease a 30 x 25 cm Swiss roll tin. Dissolve yeast in warm water. Set mixture aside 5 minutes or until frothy. Combine milk, sugar and butter in pan. Stir over medium heat until butter has melted.

2 Sift the salt and 2 1/2 cups of the flour into a large bowl; make a well in the centre of the mixture. Add the yeast, milk mixture and egg; beat until well combined.

3 Add enough of the remaining flour to form a soft dough. Turn dough onto a lightly floured surface and knead for 10 minutes or until it is smooth and elastic. Place dough in a lightly oiled bowl. Cover dough with lightly oiled plastic wrap and leave in a warm place for 1 hour or until dough is well risen. Knead dough again for 1 minute.

4 Divide dough in two, making one portion larger than the other. Roll out the larger portion to fit into the pre-pared tin; place dough in tin. Press the dough up the sides of the tin.

5 Combine the jam and water in a small pan and stir over low heat until jam is warm and slightly liquefied. Spread half of the warmed jam over the dough in the tin. Top with pie apple and the remaining jam. Roll out remaining dough to make a lid; place lid on apple mixture. Scatter the Crumble Topping thickly over the dough. Cover Streusel Kuchen and leave in a warm place about 1 hour or until well risen. Preheat oven to 210°C (190°C gas). Bake dough for 5 minutes. Reduce oven temperature to 180°C and bake for another 40–50 minutes or until dough is cooked and top is golden.

6 **To make Crumble Topping:** Combine the sugar, flour and cinnamon in small bowl; rub in butter until it resembles coarse breadcrumbs. Stir in walnuts.

COOK'S FILE

Storage time: Streusel Kuchen can be stored in an airtight container for up to 4 days. To freeze, wrap tightly in foil, place in a freezer bag and store in freezer for up to a month. Reheat in a 180°C oven for 20 minutes.

Variations: Use an 825 g can of apricot halves instead of the pie apple. Make sure to drain the apricots well before using.

• Substitute 1 cup of shredded coconut for the walnuts in Topping.

Dissolve yeast in warm water and set aside for 5 minutes or until frothy.

Make a well in the centre of the mixture and add yeast, milk mixture and egg.

Knead the dough on a lightly floured surface for 10 minutes or until elastic.

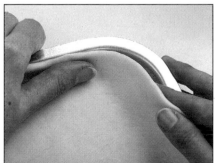
Fit the dough into the Swiss roll tin, pressing it up the sides.

Spread dough with half of the liquefied jam, then top with pie apple.

Scatter the Crumble Topping thickly over the dough.

OLD-FASHIONED DAMPER

Preparation time: 10 minutes
Total cooking time: 30–45 minutes
Serves 8

4 cups self-raising flour
1 teaspoon baking powder
1 teaspoon salt
1 tablespoon caster sugar
3/4 cup milk
1/2–3/4 cup water
30 g butter, melted
milk and flour, extra

1 Preheat oven to 210°C (190°C gas). Brush an oven tray with melted butter or oil. Sift flour, baking powder and salt into a bowl, stir in sugar and make a well in the centre. (Add extra ingredients, if using. See Variations.) Combine milk, 1/2 cup of the water and butter; add all at once to flour.
2 Using a flat-bladed knife, mix briefly and lightly to a soft and slightly sticky dough. Add the remaining water if necessary. Turn the dough out onto a lightly floured surface and knead briefly. Form dough into a rough ball.
3 Place on prepared tray, flatten slightly and brush with milk and sprinkle with a little flour. Cut a cross 1 cm deep on top of dough ball. Bake 15 minutes then reduce oven to 180°C and bake another 25–30 minutes or until golden.

VARIATIONS

Italian: Combine 1/2 cup chopped fresh basil, 3/4 cup drained and chopped sun-dried tomatoes and 12 chopped black olives. Add to the flour mixture and make dough as directed by recipe. Divide the dough into 2 portions; slash the tops.

Herb: Combine 2 cups chopped fresh herbs, such as parsley, chives, mint, dill, tarragon, basil or oregano. (Use at least three.) Add to flour mixture and make dough as directed by recipe. Divide the dough into 3 portions, shape into small ovals and sprinkle tops with 1/2 cup grated cheddar cheese.

Corn: Replace 1 cup of the self-raising flour with 1 cup fine cornmeal and 2 teaspoons baking powder. Add 310 g can drained corn kernels, 1/2 chopped capsicum, 2 finely chopped small red chillies and 1/2 cup chopped coriander. Make the dough according to the recipe. Divide dough in two; slash tops. Brush with milk and sprinkle with extra cornmeal.

Onion: Cook 1/2 cup chopped spring onions in butter. Add to flour mixture when cool with 40 g sachet French onion soup mix and 1/2 cup chopped parsley. Make the dough according to the recipe. Form dough into a large oval; make a slash along the length of the dough.

Nutty Cheese: Combine 1 cup chopped walnuts or pecans, 1 cup grated cheddar cheese and 1/2 cup of grated parmesan. Add to the flour mixture and make dough as directed by the recipe. Shape the dough into a round.

Fruit: Soak 1 1/2 cups sultanas or currants in 3/4 cup orange juice for 30 minutes. Drain, reserving juice, then combine with 2 teaspoons grated orange rind and 1 tablespoon caster sugar. Add to flour mixture and make dough as directed by recipe. Use the orange juice to moisten the dough instead of the water. Divide dough into 2 portions and score a cross into the tops.

Clockwise from top left: Old-fashioned, Italian, Corn, Nutty Cheese, Fruit, Herb and Onion Dampers

CHOCOLATE TARTS

Preparation time: 30 minutes +
  20 minutes refrigeration
Total cooking time: 15 minutes
Makes 24

2 cups plain flour
2 tablespoons custard powder
125 g butter, chopped
1 egg yolk
2–3 tablespoons iced water

Filling
250 g cream cheese, at room
  temperature
1/2 cup caster sugar
1 egg
125 g dark chocolate, melted
1/4 cup ground almonds
  or hazelnuts
100 g white chocolate, melted

1 Preheat the oven to 180°C. Brush two 12-cup shallow patty tins with melted butter or oil. Combine the flour, custard powder and butter in a food processor and then process for 30 seconds, or until the mixture is fine and crumbly. Add the egg yolk and almost all of the water and process for 20 seconds or until the mixture just comes together, adding the rest of the water if necessary. Turn the dough out onto a lightly floured surface and knead it gently until smooth. Cover and leave in the refrigerator for 20 minutes.

2 Divide the pastry dough in two; wrap one portion and set aside. Roll the other half between two sheets of baking paper to a thickness of 3 mm. Cut rounds using a 7 cm fluted cutter. Ease the pastry rounds into the prepared trays. Repeat with the other portion of pastry. Refrigerate the trays while preparing the Filling.

3 To make Filling: Using electric beaters, beat the cream cheese and sugar until light and creamy. Add the egg and cooled melted chocolate. Beat until well combined and no streaks are visible. Stir in the ground nuts. Spoon the Filling into the pastry cases. Bake for 15 minutes or until just beginning to firm. (The tarts will set more on standing.) Remove from the oven and allow to cool on a wire rack. Drizzle or pipe with white chocolate and allow to set. Sprinkle with cocoa powder to serve, if desired.

Process mixture for 30 seconds or until it is fine and crumbly.

Cut out pastry rounds with a fluted pastry cutter.

Spoon the Chocolate Filling into the pastry rounds.

LITTLE LEMON TARTS

Preparation time: 40 minutes
Total cooking time: 15 minutes
Makes about 24

2 cups plain flour
pinch salt
125 g butter, chopped
2 teaspoons caster sugar
1 teaspoon lemon rind
1 egg yolk
2–3 tablespoons iced water

Filling
125 g cream cheese, softened
1/2 cup caster sugar
2 egg yolks
2 tablespoons lemon juice
1/2 cup sweetened condensed milk

1 Preheat oven to 180°C. Brush two 12-cup patty tins with oil. Sift flour and salt into bowl. Rub butter into flour mixture. Add sugar, rind, egg yolk and water and mix with a knife. Gently knead on a lightly floured surface until smooth. Cover in plastic wrap and refrigerate 10 minutes.

2 To make Filling: Using electric beaters, beat combined cream cheese, sugar and egg yolks until smooth and thickened. Add lemon juice and condensed milk; beat until well combined.

3 Roll out dough between sheets of baking paper to 3 mm thickness. Using a 7 cm fluted, round cutter, cut rounds from pastry. Gently press pastry into patty tins. Lightly prick each round 3 times with a fork and bake 10 minutes or until just starting to turn golden. Remove from oven and spoon 2 teaspoons of Filling into each case. Return to the oven for another 5 minutes or until filling has set. Allow tarts to cool slightly before removing from tins. Garnish with candied lemon strips, if desired.

COOK'S FILE

Note: Make candied lemon strips by simmering lemon peel in sugar syrup.

Rub the butter into the flour using your fingertips.

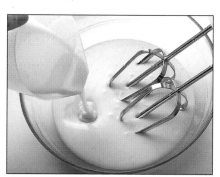

Add the lemon juice and condensed milk to the Filling mixture.

Lightly prick each pastry case three times with a fork.

APPLE STRUDELS

Preparation time: 20 minutes
Total cooking time: 20–25 minutes
Makes 2 strudels

4 green cooking apples
30 g butter
2 tablespoons orange juice
1 tablespoon honey
¼ cup sugar
½ cup sultanas
2 sheets ready-rolled puff
　pastry
¼ cup ground almonds
1 egg, lightly beaten

2 tablespoons soft brown sugar
1 teaspoon ground cinnamon

1 Preheat oven to 220°C. Brush two oven trays with melted butter or oil. Peel, core and thinly slice apples. Heat butter in a medium pan; add apples and cook 2 minutes until lightly golden. Add orange juice, honey, sugar and sultanas. Stir over medium heat until sugar dissolves and apples are just tender. Remove from heat and cool completely.
2 Place a sheet of pastry on flat work surface. Fold in half; make small cuts in folded edge of pastry at 2 cm intervals. Open out pastry and sprinkle

with half of the ground almonds. Drain away liquid from the apples and place half of the mixture in the centre of the pastry. Brush edges with egg and fold together, pressing firmly.
3 Place strudel on prepared tray seam-side down. Brush top with egg and sprinkle with half of the combined sugar and cinnamon. Repeat process with other sheet and remaining filling. Bake 20–25 minutes or until pastry is golden and crisp.

COOK'S FILE

Variation: Many types of fruit or canned fruit, such as pears, cherries or apricots, can be used for strudel.

Stir the fruit over medium heat until sugar has dissolved and apple is tender.

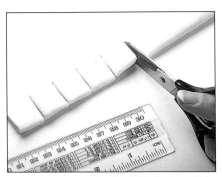

Make small cuts in the folded edge of the pastry at 2 cm intervals.

Place strudel on oven tray and sprinkle with combined sugar and cinnamon.

Combine the water and butter in a pan and stir until butter melts.

Stir mixture with a wooden spoon until it leaves the sides of the pan.

Pipe 15 cm lengths of pastry onto the prepared tray.

Split the cooked eclairs and remove any uncooked dough.

CHOCOLATE ECLAIRS

Preparation time: 20 minutes
Total cooking time: 40 minutes
Makes about 18

1 cup water
125 g butter
1 cup plain flour, sifted
4 eggs
300 ml cream, whipped
150 g dark chocolate, melted

1 Preheat oven to 210°C (190°C gas). Brush two baking trays with oil. Combine water and butter in small pan. Stir over medium heat until butter melts. Bring to the boil, then remove from heat.

2 Add flour all at once. Return to heat and stir with a wooden spoon until mixture leaves the sides of the pan and forms a ball around the spoon. Transfer mixture to a large bowl. Cool slightly. Add eggs one at a time, beating well after each addition, until mixture is thick, smooth and shiny.

3 Spoon mixture into a piping bag fitted with a 1.5 cm plain nozzle. Pipe 15 cm lengths onto prepared trays, leaving room for expansion.

4 Bake for 10–15 minutes. Reduce heat to 180°C. Bake for another 15 minutes or until golden and firm. Split each eclair, removing any uncooked dough. Fill puffs with cream. Coat the tops liberally with melted chocolate.

COOK'S FILE

Storage time: Freeze unfilled eclairs in an airtight container for up to 3 months.

STRAWBERRY CREAM TARTS

Preparation time: 30 minutes
Total cooking time: 15 minutes
Makes 24

2 cups plain flour
¼ cup icing sugar
150 g butter, chopped
2–3 tablespoons iced water

Filling
1 cup cream
1 tablespoon icing sugar
1 teaspoon vanilla essence

250 g strawberries, hulled and quartered

1 Preheat oven to 180°C. Brush two 12-cup patty tins with oil. Sift flour and icing sugar into bowl. Add butter; rub in, using fingertips, until mixture is crumbly. Add almost all the water; mix to a dough with a flat-bladed knife, adding more water if necessary.

2 Turn out onto a lightly floured surface, press together until smooth. Roll out between sheets of baking paper to 3 mm thickness. Using a fluted biscuit cutter, cut out circles to fit prepared tins. Ease pastry into tins; refrigerate for 15 minutes.

3 Prick pastry cases twice with a fork. Bake 10–15 minutes or until golden. Cool; remove from trays and cool completely on a wire rack.

To make Filling: Using electric beaters, whip cream, icing sugar and essence until firm peaks form. Stir strawberries though the mixture. Spoon into pastry cases. Serve within 2 hours of filling.

COOK'S FILE

Storage time: Tart cases can be made up to 1 day in advance; store in an airtight container.
Variation: Use raspberries, blue berries or any other fruit in season.

Using a knife, mix to a dough, adding more water if necessary.

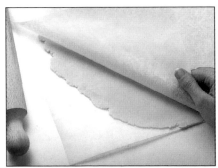

Roll out pastry between two sheets of baking paper.

Whip the cream with electric beaters until firm peaks form.

JAM AND CREAM SPONGE

Preparation time: 20 minutes
Total cooking time: 20 minutes
Makes one 20 cm round cake

1/2 cup plain flour
1/2 cup self-raising flour
4 eggs, separated
2/3 cup caster sugar
1/2 cup strawberry jam
1/2 cup cream, whipped
icing sugar, for dusting

1 Preheat oven to 180°C. Brush two shallow 20 cm sandwich tins with oil or melted butter. Sift the flours three times onto greaseproof paper. Place the egg whites in a large bowl. Using electric beaters, beat whites until firm peaks form. Add sugar gradually, beating constantly until sugar has completely dissolved and mixture is thick and glossy.

2 Add egg yolks and beat for another 20 seconds. Using a metal spoon, fold in flour quickly and lightly. Spread mixture evenly into prepared tins; smooth surface. Bake 20 minutes,

until lightly golden and springy to the touch. Leave cakes in tins 5 minutes before turning onto wire racks to cool.

3 Spread jam evenly onto one of the sponges. Spread whipped cream over the jam. Top with the second sponge and dust with sifted icing sugar before serving.

COOK'S FILE

Storage time: Unfilled sponges can be frozen for up to a month; freeze in separate bags. Thaw cakes at room temperature for 20 minutes. Filled sponge is best served immediately.

Using electric beaters, beat the mixture until it is thick and glossy.

Spread mixture into tins and smooth the surface with a flat-bladed knife.

Dust the filled sponge with sifted icing sugar.

COFFEE LIQUEUR GATEAU

Preparation time: 1 hour
Total cooking time: 35–40 minutes
Serves 8–10

125 g brazil nuts
100 g blanched almonds
80 g hazelnuts
2 tablespoons plain flour
3/4 cup caster sugar
7 egg whites
1/4 cup Tia Maria or Kahlua
small chocolate buttons, for
    decoration
sifted icing sugar,
    for dusting

Coffee Cream
200 g butter
150 g dark chocolate, melted
2–3 teaspoons icing sugar
2 teaspoons warm water
3–4 teaspoons instant coffee
    powder

1 Preheat oven to moderate 180°C. Brush a deep 20 cm round tin with melted butter or oil. Line base and sides with baking paper. Place nuts on an oven tray. Roast 5–10 minutes or until golden. Rub nuts vigorously in a clean tea towel to remove hazelnut skins. Place nuts in a food processor; process until finely ground.

2 Transfer nuts to a large bowl; add flour and 1/2 cup of the sugar; mix well. Using electric beaters, beat egg whites in large bowl until soft peaks form. Gradually add remaining sugar, beating until mixture is thick and glossy and sugar is dissolved. Using a metal spoon, fold nut mixture into egg

mixture a third at a time. Spoon into the prepared tin; smooth surface. Bake for 35–40 minutes or until springy to the touch. Leave cake in the tin to cool completely.

3 To make Coffee Cream: Beat butter in small bowl with electric beaters until light and creamy. Gradually pour in melted chocolate; beating until well combined. Add icing sugar and combined water and coffee; beat until smooth.

4 To assemble Gateau: Turn cake onto a flat working surface. Using a sharp serrated knife, carefully cut cake horizontally into three layers. (Use top layer of cake as base of gateau.) Brush first layer with half the liqueur. Spread with one fifth of the Coffee Cream.

5 Place second cake layer on top. Brush with remaining liqueur and spread with a quarter of the remaining Cream. Place remaining layer on top. Spread top and sides with the remaining Cream.

6 Decorate the top of the cake with chocolate buttons. Dust with icing sugar. Refrigerate for 1 hour or until firm.

COOK'S FILE

Note: Small chocolate buttons can be made at home with 150 g of melted chocolate melts. Line two trays with baking paper. Place half the chocolate in small paper icing bag. Seal end of bag, then snip off tip. Pipe small chocolate buttons onto trays. Tap trays lightly on bench to flatten buttons. Allow chocolate to set. Peel off paper and use to decorate.

Storage time: Coffee Liqueur Gateau can be prepared up to three days in advance. Keep refrigerated in an airtight container.

To remove skins, rub the roasted nuts vigorously with a tea towel.

Using a metal spoon, fold nut mixture into egg whites a third at a time.

Gradually add the melted chocolate to the butter while beating continuously.

Use a serrated knife to slice the cake into three even layers.

Brush the cake layers with liqueur, then spread with Coffee Cream.

Decorate the top of the cake lavishly with chocolate buttons.

CARROT AND PINEAPPLE CAKE

Preparation time: 20 minutes
Total cooking time: 40 minutes
Makes one 20 cm cake

1 cup plain flour
1 teaspoon baking powder
1/2 teaspoon bicarbonate of soda
1/2 teaspoon ground cinnamon
1/2 teaspoon ground nutmeg
2/3 cup soft brown sugar
1/4 cup oil
2 eggs
1 cup grated carrot

440 g can crushed pineapple, drained
1/4 cup chopped pecans

Frosting
60 g butter
60 g cream cheese
1 cup icing sugar
1 teaspoon orange juice
1/2 teaspoon vanilla essence

1 Preheat oven to 180°C. Brush a 20 cm round cake tin with oil or melted butter; line base and side with baking paper. Sift flour, baking powder, soda, cinnamon and nutmeg into a bowl. Add sugar and stir to combine. Make a well in the centre. Whisk oil and eggs until pale and smooth; stir into flour mixture.

2 Add carrot, pineapple and pecans to mixture and stir to combine. Spoon mixture into prepared tin; smooth surface. Bake 35–40 minutes or until skewer comes out clean when inserted into centre of cake.

3 Cool cake in tin 5 minutes before turning out onto a wire rack to cool completely. Spread cake with Frosting. Decorate with orange rind, if desired.

To make Frosting: Using electric beaters, beat butter and cream cheese until smooth. Add icing sugar, juice and vanilla and beat well.

Sift the flour, baking powder, soda, cinnamon and nutmeg into a bowl.

Add carrot, pineapple and pecans to cake batter and stir.

Spread the cake with a thick layer of Frosting.

RICH CHOCOLATE CAKE

Preparation time: 20 minutes +
  30 minutes standing
Total cooking time: 50–60 minutes
Makes one 20 cm round cake

125 g butter
1 cup caster sugar
2 eggs, lightly beaten
1 teaspoon vanilla essence
1/3 cup self-raising flour
1 cup plain flour
1 teaspoon bicarbonate of soda
1/2 cup cocoa powder
3/4 cup buttermilk

Icing
1/2 cup icing sugar
2 tablespoons cocoa powder
1 tablespoon milk, warmed
25 g butter, softened

1 Preheat oven to 180°C. Brush a 20 cm round cake tin with melted butter or oil. Line base and side with baking paper. Using electric beaters, beat butter and sugar until light and creamy. Add eggs gradually, beating continuously. Add essence and beat until well combined.

2 Transfer mixture to bowl. Using a metal spoon, fold in sifted flours, soda and cocoa powder alternately with the buttermilk. Stir the mixture until combined and smooth. Spoon the mixture into the prepared tin; smooth the surface.

3 Bake 50–60 minutes or until a skewer comes out clean when inserted into centre of cake. Leave cake in tin 30 minutes before turning onto wire rack to cool. Top with Icing.

To make Icing: Combine the sifted icing sugar and cocoa in a small bowl. Add milk and butter; stir until smooth.

COOK'S FILE

Storage time: Store cake in an airtight container for several days.

Add the eggs gradually, beating continuously.

Using a metal spoon, lightly fold in flours, soda and cocoa powder.

Turn cake out onto wire rack after 30 minutes of cooling.

FRUIT MINCE AND NUT CAKE

Preparation time: 40 minutes +
  3 hours standing
Total cooking time: 3–3 hours and
  30 minutes
Makes one 20 cm round cake

1 1/2 cups plain flour
1/2 cup self-raising flour
1 teaspoon mixed spice
3/4 cup soft brown sugar
1 cup raisins
1 cup sultanas

100 g mixed raw nuts, chopped
200 g pecans
250 g butter, melted and cooled
425 g ready-made fruit mince
1 green apple, peeled and grated
2 tablespoons orange marmalade
2 tablespoons rum
2 eggs, lightly beaten

1 Preheat oven to 160°C. Brush a 20 cm round cake tin with oil or melted butter; line base and side with baking paper. Line outside of tin with a double thickness of brown paper; secure with string.
2 Sift flours and mixed spice into a bowl. Add sugar, raisins, sultanas and nuts, reserving half of the pecans. Make a well in the centre. Add butter, mince, apple, marmalade, rum and egg; stir until well combined.
3 Spoon mixture evenly into prepared tin; smooth surface. Decorate with reserved pecans. Bake for 3–3 1/2 hours or until skewer comes out clean when inserted in centre of cake. Allow cake to cool in tin several hours or overnight before turning out.

COOK'S FILE

Storage time: Store in an airtight container for up to one month.

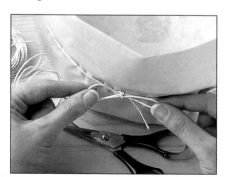

Wrap tin with double thickness of brown paper; secure with string.

Once all the ingredients have been added, stir well to combine.

Decorate the top of the cake with the reserved pecans.

Cover fruits and liqueur with plastic wrap and allow to stand overnight.

Stir semolina over low heat until it is lightly browned.

Add the marmalade, honey, orange rind and juice; beat until combined.

Spoon the batter into the prepared tin and smooth the surface.

SEMOLINA FRUIT CAKE

Preparation time: 20 minutes +
overnight standing
Total cooking time: 4 hours
Makes one 23 cm round cake

1½ cups dried mixed fruit
1½ cups sultanas, finely
   chopped
⅓ cup mixed peel, finely
   chopped
½ cup finely chopped dried figs
1 cup finely chopped combined
   glacé fruit
½ cup currants
½ cup glacé ginger, finely
   chopped
½ cup Grand Marnier
1½ cups semolina
½ teaspoon ground cinnamon
½ teaspoon mixed spice
1 teaspoon ground cardamom
185 g butter
4 eggs
1 cup soft brown sugar
½ cup marmalade
¼ cup honey
3 teaspoons grated orange rind
⅓ cup orange juice
1 cup slivered almonds

1 Combine dried fruit, sultanas, peel, figs, glacé fruit, currants, ginger and Grand Marnier in a bowl, cover with plastic wrap; stand overnight.
2 Stir semolina in a pan 5 minutes or until browned. Add spices and butter; stir until butter has melted. Cover with plastic wrap, set aside overnight.
3 Brush a deep 23 cm round cake tin with melted butter or oil; line base and side with baking paper. Line outside of tin with a double thickness of brown paper; secure with string. Preheat oven to 150°C. Using electric beaters, beat eggs and sugar in small bowl until pale and foamy. Add marmalade, honey, orange rind and juice; beat until combined. Transfer to a large bowl; add fruits, semolina mixture and almonds. Using a metal spoon, stir until just combined.
4 Spoon mixture into prepared tin; smooth surface. Bake 1 hour. Cover cake with foil, reduce heat to 120°C. Bake 3 hours or until cake is golden brown; cool in tin completely before turning out onto a serving plate.

COOK'S FILE

Note: Store cake in a cool dark place in an airtight container for up to three months.

ORANGE BERRY SPONGE

Preparation time: 50 minutes
Total cooking time: 40 minutes
Serves 6–8

½ cup plain flour
¼ cup cornflour
1 teaspoon baking powder
¼ cup milk
50 g butter
¾ cup caster sugar
3 eggs
3 egg yolks
1 teaspoon finely grated
    orange rind
1½ cups cream
3–4 teaspoons icing sugar
1–2 tablespoons Grand
    Marnier
250 g strawberries, hulled
    and sliced
250 g blueberries
2 tablespoons flaked almonds,
    toasted
icing sugar, for dusting

1 Preheat oven to 180°C. Brush a 30 x 20 cm lamington tin (or equivalent) with melted butter or oil. Line base and sides with baking paper extending 3 cm over each edge. Sift flours and baking powder twice onto a sheet of greaseproof paper. Place milk and butter in pan. Stir over medium heat until butter has melted. (Do not boil the mixture but keep it hot.)

2 Place sugar, eggs and yolks in large heatproof bowl. Stand bowl over a pan of simmering water. Using electric beaters, beat mixture over heat until pale yellow, thick and glossy and increased in volume. Remove bowl from heat. Stir in rind until well combined.

3 Using a metal spoon, fold in a third of the flour at a time. Fold in hot butter mixture and stir until just smooth. (Do not over-mix. It is important to keep as much volume as possible in the mixture.) Spoon mixture into prepared tin. Bake 25–30 minutes or until springy to the touch. Leave cake in tin to cool.

4 Turn cake out onto a flat work surface. Using a sharp serrated knife, trim cake of any dark patches. Cut cake into three even rectangles (around 10 x 20 cm each).

5 Beat cream and icing sugar with electric beaters until stiff peaks form. Stir in Grand Marnier.

6 Spread one quarter of the cream mixture over one layer of cake. Top with a third of the berries. Add a second layer of cake; press down lightly. Repeat process with cream and berries, reserving some berries for the top and finishing with third cake layer. Spread remaining cream evenly over top and sides of cake. Decorate cake with remaining berries and toasted flaked almonds. Dust cake lightly with icing sugar.

COOK'S FILE

Storage time: Sponge cake can be made up to 2 days in advance. Store covered tightly with plastic wrap, in a cool dry place. Assemble cake up to two hours prior to serving.

Note: To toast almonds scatter on an oven tray lined with baking paper. Place in preheated 180°C oven for 5–10 minutes.

Variations: Do not use frozen or canned berries in this recipe—they are too soggy. If blueberries are unavailable, substitute with any berry in season, such as blackberries, or omit second berry entirely, if you prefer.

Line the base and sides of a lamington tin with baking paper.

Beat sugar and egg mixture over simmering water until thick and glossy.

Fold in the hot butter mixture and stir lightly until just smooth.

Place cooked sponge on a sheet of baking paper and cut into 3 even rectangles.

Beat the cream and the icing sugar until stiff peaks form.

Top second layer with cream and berries, reserving some berries for the top.

PIKELETS

Preparation time: 10 minutes
Total cooking time: 15 minutes
Makes about 25

½ teaspoon lemon
   juice
¾ cup milk
1 cup self-raising flour
¼ teaspoon bicarbonate
   of soda
2 tablespoons caster
   sugar
1 egg, lightly beaten
30 g butter, melted

1 Combine the lemon juice and the milk in a small bowl and set aside for 5 minutes. Sift the flour and bicarbonate of soda into a medium bowl; add the sugar and stir until combined. Make a well in the centre.

2 Add the egg and ½ cup of the milk mixture all at once. Using a wooden spoon, stir to a smooth batter until all the liquid is incorporated and the batter is free of lumps (but do not over-beat). Add more milk if the batter does not drop easily from the spoon.

3 Brush the base of a frying pan with a little of the melted butter. Drop heaped teaspoonfuls of the mixture in the pan about 3 cm apart. Cook over medium heat for 2 minutes or until bubbles begin to form on the top. Turn the pikelets over and cook the other side. Remove from the pan; repeat the process with the remaining mixture. Serve topped with jam and whipped cream, if desired.

COOK'S FILE

Note: Combining the lemon juice (an acid) with the milk for the batter will cause the milk to 'sour' and thicken slightly when left for a few minutes. This modified milk will make lighter pikelets, but plain milk can also be used if your time is short. Do not be alarmed if the milk looks curdled after combining with the lemon juice.

Below, left to right: Pikelets; Pikelets topped with jam and cream; Currant and Tea Pikelets

CURRANT AND TEA PIKELETS

Preparation time: 20 minutes
Total cooking time: 15 minutes
Makes about 20

½ cup hot strong black tea
2 tablespoons currants
1 cup self-raising flour
2 tablespoons caster sugar
1 egg, lightly beaten
30 g butter, melted

1 Combine tea and currants in a small mixing bowl. Allow to stand for 10 minutes or until tea has cooled and currants are plump.
2 Sift flour into a medium bowl. Add sugar and stir until combined. Make a well in the centre.
3 Add tea mixture and egg to flour all at once. Stir, using a wooden spoon, until all the liquid is incorporated and batter is free of lumps.
4 Brush the base of a frying pan lightly with a little of the butter. Drop level tablespoons of the mixture in pan about 3 cm apart. Cook over medium heat for 2–3 minutes or until bubbles appear on the surface. Turn over and cook other side. Repeat with remaining batter. Serve with whipped cream, if desired.

COOK'S FILE

Note: For these pikelets, use quite a strongly flavoured tea such as any China tea, Earl Grey or English Breakfast tea. Herbal teas, which do not contain tannin, are unsuitable.

Add the egg to the mixture and beat well with electric beaters.

Add pecans and cherries and stir with a metal spoon.

Arrange the pear slices decoratively on the top of the cake.

Turn the cake out onto a wire rack and allow it to cool.

PEAR AND PECAN TEACAKE

Preparation time: 20 minutes
Total cooking time: 1 hour
Makes one 23 cm cake

60 g butter
3/4 **cup caster sugar**
1 **egg**
2 **cups self-raising flour, sifted**
1/2 **cup milk**
1/2 **cup chopped pecans**
1/4 **cup chopped glacé cherries**
2 **pears, peeled, cored**
   and sliced
1 **tablespoon cinnamon sugar**
   (See Note)

1 Preheat the oven to 180°C. Brush a 23 cm round cake tin with oil or melted butter and then line the base with non-stick baking paper. Using electric beaters, beat the butter and sugar until the mixture is creamy. Add the egg and beat well.

2 Lightly fold in the flour alternately with the milk, finishing with the flour. Add the pecans and cherries and stir until just combined.

3 Spoon the mixture into the prepared tin and smooth the surface. Arrange the slices of pear decoratively over the top of the teacake and then sprinkle generously with the cinnamon sugar.

4 Bake for 1 hour in the preheated oven, or until a skewer comes out clean when inserted into the centre of the teacake. Leave the cake to cool in the tin for about 5 minutes before turning out onto a wire rack to cool completely.

COOK'S FILE

Note: To make cinnamon sugar combine 1 tablespoon caster sugar with 1/2 teaspoon ground cinnamon.

CINNAMON TEACAKE

Preparation time: 20 minutes
Total cooking time: 30 minutes
Makes one 20 cm cake

60 g butter
1/2 cup caster sugar
1 egg, lightly beaten
1 teaspoon vanilla essence
3/4 cup self-raising flour
1/4 cup plain flour
1/2 cup milk
20 g butter, melted

1 tablespoon caster sugar, extra
1 teaspoon ground cinnamon

1 Preheat oven to 180°C. Brush a 20 cm round cake tin with oil or melted butter; line the base with baking paper. Using electric beaters, beat the butter and sugar in a small bowl until light and creamy. Add the beaten egg gradually, beating well after each addition. Add vanilla essence and beat until combined.

2 Transfer the mixture to a large bowl. Using a metal spoon, fold in sifted flours, alternately with milk.

Stir until smooth. Spoon into prepared tin and smooth the surface. Bake for 30 minutes or until a skewer comes out clean when inserted into the centre of the cake. Stand cake in tin for 5 minutes before turning out onto a wire rack to cool.

3 Brush the cake with melted butter while still warm. Sprinkle the cake with the combined extra sugar and cinnamon.

COOK'S FILE

Storage time: Cake can be frozen for up to 3 months.

Brush cake tin with melted butter or oil and line base with baking paper.

Lightly fold in the sifted flours alternately with the milk.

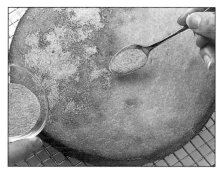

Sprinkle the cooked cake liberally with combined sugar and cinnamon.

97

APPLE AND SPICE TEACAKE

Preparation time: 35 minutes
Total cooking time: 1 hour
Makes one 20 cm cake

180 g butter
1/2 cup soft brown sugar
2 teaspoons finely grated
    lemon rind
3 eggs, lightly beaten
1 cup self-raising flour
1/2 cup wholemeal flour
1/2 teaspoon cinnamon

1/2 cup milk
410 g can pie apple
1/4 teaspoon ground mixed spice
1 tablespoon soft brown
    sugar, extra
1/4 cup flaked almonds

1 Preheat oven to moderate 180°C. Brush a 20 cm springform pan with oil or melted butter; line base with paper. Using electric beaters, beat butter and sugar until light and creamy. Beat in rind. Add egg gradually, beating well after each addition.

2 Fold sifted flours and cinnamon into creamed mixture alternately with milk. Spoon half of the mixture into the prepared tin, top with three-quarters of the pie apple then top with remaining cake batter. Press the remaining pie apple around the edge of the top. Combine the mixed spice, extra sugar and flaked almonds and sprinkle over cake.

3 Bake 1 hour or until skewer comes out clean when inserted in the centre of cake. Remove from tin and cool on a wire rack.

COOK'S FILE

Variation: Pie apricots can be used instead of apples if desired.

Cream the butter and sugar, then add the grated lemon rind.

Spoon apple onto half the batter and top with remaining batter.

The cake is cooked when a skewer comes out clean.

PASSIONFRUIT BUTTER TEACAKE

Preparation time: 20 minutes +
  1 hour refrigeration
Total cooking time: 45 minutes
Serves 8

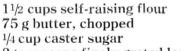

1½ cups self-raising flour
75 g butter, chopped
¼ cup caster sugar
2 teaspoons finely grated lemon
  rind
2 tablespoons lemon juice
1 tablespoon water

Filling
1 cup caster sugar
4 eggs
⅔ cup passionfruit pulp (6–8)
125 g butter, chopped

Topping
60 g butter, chopped
¼ cup soft brown sugar
½ cup self-raising flour

1 Combine flour and butter in a food processor. Process until the mixture becomes fine and crumbly. Add the sugar, lemon rind and juice. Process until mixture comes together, adding the water if necessary. Wrap the dough in plastic wrap and refrigerate for 1 hour.
2 To Make Filling: Combine sugar, eggs, pulp and butter in a pan. Whisk constantly, over low heat, until butter has melted; cool. Preheat oven to 210°C (190°C gas). Brush a 23 cm springform tin with oil or melted butter; line base with baking paper. Press dough out to line base of prepared pan. Bake for 15 minutes. Remove from oven and spread Filling evenly over cake. Reduce oven to 180°C and bake another 15 minutes. Sprinkle Topping on cake and place under a pre-heated grill until golden. Allow to cool before releasing from tin.
3 To make Topping: Using electric beaters, beat butter and sugar until light and creamy. Add flour and stir through until mixture becomes soft and crumbly.

COOK'S FILE

Storage time: Store in an airtight container for several days.

Process the flour and the butter until it is fine and crumbly.

Whisk Filling mixture constantly over low heat until butter melts.

Place cake with Topping under hot grill until top becomes golden.

DATE-WALNUT LOAVES

Preparation time: 25 minutes
Total cooking time: 1 hour
Makes two loaves

³/4 cup self-raising flour
³/4 cup plain flour
¹/2 teaspoon bicarbonate
  of soda
1 teaspoon mixed spice
1 cup chopped walnuts
100 g butter
³/4 cup soft brown sugar
¹/2 cup water
1¹/2 cups chopped dates
1 egg, lightly beaten

1 Preheat the oven to 180°C. Brush two 17 x 8 cm tube tins (nut-roll tins) and their lids with oil or melted butter. Sift the flours, soda and spice into a large bowl. Add the walnuts and stir to combine. Make a well in the centre of the mixture.
2 Combine the butter, sugar, water and dates in a pan. Stir continuously over low heat until the butter has melted and the sugar has dissolved. Remove from the heat and leave to cool slightly. Add the butter mixture and egg to the flour mixture and stir until combined.
3 Spoon the mixture evenly into the prepared tins. Bake, with the tins upright, for 1 hour, or until a skewer comes out clean when inserted into the centre of the loaves. Leave the loaves in their tins, with the lids on, for 10 minutes, then turn out onto a wire rack to cool.

COOK'S FILE

Storage time: Store in an airtight container for up to three days.

Make a well in the centre of the flour mixture with a wooden spoon.

Combine butter, sugar, water and dates and stir over low heat.

Spoon the mixture into the prepared nut-roll tins.

HONEY, NUT AND FRUIT LOAF

Preparation time: 20 minutes
Total cooking time: 1 hour
Makes one loaf

1 cup honey
45 g butter
1 egg
2½ cups self-raising flour
½ teaspoon bicarbonate of soda
½ teaspoon ground cinnamon
¾ cup milk

½ cup chopped pecans
¼ cup chopped almonds
¼ cup chopped pitted prunes
¼ cup chopped dried
   apricots
¼ cup raisins

1 Preheat oven to 180°C. Brush a 15 x 23 cm loaf tin with oil or melted butter; line base with baking paper. Using electric beaters, beat honey and butter until well combined. Add egg and beat well. Transfer mixture to a large bowl.
2 Fold sifted flour, bicarbonate of soda and cinnamon into creamed mixture alternately with milk. Fold in nuts and fruit.
3 Spoon mixture into prepared tin; smooth surface. Bake for 45 minutes; cover cake with foil and bake for another 15 minutes or until skewer comes out clean when inserted in centre of cake. Cool cake in tin 10 minutes before turning out onto a wire rack to cool completely.

COOK'S FILE

Storage time: Store in an airtight container for up to three days.

Mark the baking paper to fit using the bar tin as a guide.

Lightly fold in the chopped nuts and the chopped fruit.

Spoon mixture into the prepared tin and smooth the surface.

MIXED FRUIT LOAVES

Preparation time: 15 minutes +
 3 hours standing
Total cooking time: 1 hour
Makes 2 loaves

2 cups mixed dried fruit
1 cup demerara (or soft
    brown) sugar
1 cup warm black tea
4 cups self-raising flour
2 teaspoons mixed spice
1/3 cup chopped glacé cherries,
    ginger or apricots
1/2 cup chopped walnuts
2 eggs, lightly beaten
2 tablespoons golden syrup

1 Brush two 10 x 20 cm loaf tins with oil or melted butter; line bases with baking paper. Combine fruit, sugar and tea in a bowl. Cover bowl with plastic wrap. Set aside for several hours or overnight to allow flavours to combine.

2 Preheat oven to 160°C. Sift flour and mixed spice into a large bowl; add cherries and walnuts and stir to combine. Add combined egg and syrup, then fruit mixture; stir to combine.

3 Spoon mixture into prepared tins; smooth surface. Bake for 50–60 minutes or until a skewer inserted into the centre of the cake comes out clean. Allow to cool in tins for 10 minutes before turning out onto a wire rack to cool completely. Dust with icing sugar, if desired.

COOK'S FILE

Storage: This cake stores well in an airtight container. Alternatively, place in freezer bag or wrap in foil. Seal well, label and freeze.

Combine fruit, sugar and tea in a bowl, then set aside for several hours.

Add the combined egg and golden syrup to the flour mixture.

Test the cake with a skewer; it is cooked when the skewer comes out clean.

CHERRY SLICE

Preparation time: 15 minutes
Total cooking time: 35 minutes
Makes about 24

2 cups plain flour
1/2 cup icing sugar
250 g butter, chopped

Topping
30 g butter
1/3 cup caster sugar
1 tablespoon milk

2 teaspoons vanilla essence
3/4 cup chopped hazelnuts
3/4 cup sliced red glacé cherries

1 Preheat oven to 210°C (190°C gas). Brush an 18 x 28 cm shallow tin with oil or melted butter. Line base with baking paper, extending over two sides. Sift flour and icing sugar into a bowl. Add butter; rub in, using fingertips, until mixture forms a dough. Press mixture into prepared tin. Bake for 15 minutes or until light golden brown. Transfer to wire rack to cool.
2 To make Topping: Melt butter in a small pan; add sugar, milk and vanilla. Stir, without boiling, until sugar dissolves then bring to the boil. Remove from heat. Add hazelnuts and cherries to mixture and stir.
3 Spread Topping over prepared base. Bake 15 20 minutes or until golden. Cut into squares while still warm. Allow to cool.

COOK'S FILE

Variation: Melt 50 g of dark chocolate in a bowl placed over a pan of gently simmering water. Drizzle chocolate over the cooled slice.

Press the mixture into the prepared tin using your hands.

Melt the butter in a pan, then add sugar and vanilla essence.

Cut the slice into squares while it is still warm.

APPLE AND CINNAMON SLICE

Preparation time: 15 minutes
Total cooking time: 40 minutes
Makes about 36

125 g butter
1/2 cup caster sugar
2 eggs
2 cups self-raising flour, sifted
1 1/4 cups sour cream

2 green apples, peeled, cored and sliced
1/2 cup finely chopped pecans
2 tablespoons caster sugar
1 teaspoon ground cinnamon

1 Preheat oven to 180°C. Brush a 20 x 30 cm shallow tin with oil or melted butter; line base and side with baking paper, extending over two sides. Using electric beaters, beat butter and sugar until light and creamy.

Add eggs one at a time, beating well after each addition. Transfer to a bowl.
2 Using a metal spoon, fold in flour. Add sour cream and stir to combine. Spoon mixture into prepared tin.
3 Arrange apples over slice base. Sprinkle with combined pecans, sugar and cinnamon. Bake 35–40 minutes. Allow to cool in tin. Cut into squares.

COOK'S FILE

Variation: Chopped nuts can be added to the base of the slice.

Line the cake tin with baking paper so that paper extends over the sides.

Add the sour cream to the mixture and stir to combine.

Arrange apples over slice base and sprinkle with pecan mixture.

CONTINENTAL SLICE

Preparation time. 25 minutes +
4 hours refrigeration
Total cooking time: 10 minutes
Makes about 36

125 g butter
1/2 cup caster sugar
1/4 cup cocoa
250 g shredded wheat biscuits,
    crushed
3/4 cup desiccated coconut
1/4 cup chopped hazelnuts
1/4 cup chopped glacé
    cherries
1 egg, lightly beaten
1 teaspoon vanilla essence

Topping
60 g butter
1 3/4 cups icing sugar
2 tablespoons custard powder
1 tablespoon hot water
1 tablespoon Grand Marnier
125 g dark chocolate
60 g white vegetable shortening
    (copha)

1 Line base and sides of an
18 x 28 cm shallow tin with foil.
Combine butter, sugar and cocoa in a
small pan. Stir over low heat until
butter melts and mixture is well combined. Cook, stirring, 1 minute.
Remove from heat and cool slightly.
Combine biscuit crumbs, coconut,
hazelnuts and cherries in a large bowl.

Make a well in the centre; add butter
mixture, egg and vanilla all at once
and stir well. Press mixture firmly,
with the back of a spoon, into prepared tin. Refrigerate until firm.

2 To make Topping: Using electric beaters, beat butter until creamy.
Gradually add icing sugar and custard powder, alternately with water
and Grand Marnier. Beat mixture
until light and fluffy. Spread evenly
over base. Refrigerate until set.

3 Combine chocolate and shortening
in heatproof bowl; stand bowl over a
pan of simmering water and stir over
low heat until chocolate melts and
mixture is smooth. Spread over slice.
Refrigerate until firm. Cut slice into
small squares to serve.

*Using the back of a spoon, press the slice
base firmly into the tin.*

*Gradually add the icing sugar to the
creamed butter and sugar.*

*Spread the chocolate topping evenly over
the chilled slice base.*

FRUIT AND OAT SLICE

Preparation time: 20 minutes +
 10 minutes standing
Total cooking time: 1 hour
Serves 8

125 g butter
1/2 cup soft brown sugar
2 eggs, separated
1 cup wholemeal self-raising
 flour
1/4 cup wheatgerm
1/4 cup finely chopped dried
 apricots
1/4 cup boiling water
425 g can pie apple
1 small zucchini, grated
1/2 cup rolled oats
1/2 cup desiccated coconut
2 tablespoons honey

1 Preheat oven to 180°C. Brush a 20 x 30 cm shallow tin with oil or melted butter. Line the base and sides with baking paper. Using electric beaters, beat butter and sugar in a large bowl until light and creamy. Add egg yolks and beat until combined. Sift flour into mixture, return husks and mix with a flat-bladed knife. Add wheatgerm and form into a soft dough. Press mixture over base of prepared tin; smooth the surface. Bake for 12–15 minutes or until golden.
2 Soak apricots in boiling water for 10 minutes or until apricots are plump and almost all the liquid is absorbed. Spread apple over prepared base. Combine undrained apricots with zucchini, oats, coconut and honey in a bowl. Beat egg whites until stiff and fold into mixture with a metal spoon.

3 Spoon mixture over prepared base and smooth the surface. Bake slice 40–45 minutes or until golden. Leave slice to cool in pan. When cool, cut into slices to serve.

COOK'S FILE

Note: Pie apple has been used in this recipe for ease and convenience but, if desired, freshly cooked apples may be used instead.

Mix the dough with a flat-bladed knife until well combined.

Fold the egg whites into the mixture with a metal spoon.

Bake the slice for 40–45 minutes or until it is golden.

COFFEE KISSES

Preparation time: 30 minutes
Total cooking time: 10 minutes
Makes about 30

3 cups self-raising flour
160 g butter, chopped
1/2 cup caster sugar
1 egg, lightly beaten
1 tablespoon coffee powder
1–2 tablespoons iced water

Coffee Buttercream
80 g butter
1 cup icing sugar, sifted

2 teaspoons water
2 teaspoons coffee powder
100 g white chocolate, melted

1 Preheat oven to 180°C. Brush two biscuit trays with oil. Line with baking paper. Sift flour into a bowl. Add butter and rub into flour, using your fingertips, until it resembles fine breadcrumbs. Add combined sugar, egg and coffee powder, dissolved in water, all at once. Mix with a flat bladed knife until ingredients come together to form a soft dough. Lightly knead until smooth.

2 Roll out dough between two sheets of baking paper to 4 mm thickness.

Cut into 5 cm rounds, using a fluted biscuit cutter. Place on prepared trays. Bake 10 minutes or until lightly golden. Transfer biscuits to a wire rack to cool.

3 To make Coffee Buttercream: Using electric beaters, beat butter and icing sugar until light and creamy. Add combined water and coffee powder and beat until combined. Place mixture in a piping bag fitted with a fluted nozzle and pipe Buttercream onto half of the biscuits. Top with another biscuit and sandwich together. Drizzle or pipe with melted chocolate. Top with a chocolate-coated coffee bean, if desired.

Rub the butter into the flour using your fingertips.

Transfer the cooked biscuits to a wire rack to cool.

Using a bag with a fluted nozzle, pipe Coffee Buttercream on biscuits.

DRIED FRUIT PILLOWS

Preparation time: 20 minutes
  + 30 minutes refrigeration
Total cooking time:15 minutes
Makes 20

250 g cream cheese, softened
125 g butter
1½ cups plain flour
¼ cup self-raising flour
1 egg, lightly beaten, for glazing

Filling
2 tablespoons sugar
½ cup orange juice
1 teaspoon finely grated
  orange rind
1½ cups dried fruit medley
½ teaspoon ground cinnamon

1 Preheat oven to 210°C (190°C gas). Line two oven trays with baking paper. Combine cream cheese and butter in food processor. Process 20 seconds or until cream cheese and butter have combined. Add the sifted flours; process another 30 seconds or until the mixture comes together to form a soft dough. Turn dough out onto a lightly floured surface and lightly knead until smooth. Leave dough, covered with plastic wrap, in refrigerator for 30 minutes.

2 To make Filling: Combine sugar and orange juice in a small pan. Stir over low heat until sugar has dissolved. Add rind, dried fruit and bring to the boil; reduce heat and simmer, uncovered, for 5 minutes or until the fruit has softened and absorbed the liquid; allow to cool.

3 Divide pastry in two. Roll one portion of pastry between two sheets of baking paper to 4 mm thickness.

Using a knife or pastry wheel, cut dough into 8 cm squares. Brush pastry with beaten egg. Spoon a teaspoon of cooled fruit mixture onto half the square. Bring over and press together to form a pillow shape; brush tops with egg. Repeat with remaining pastry and Filling. Place pillows on prepared trays and bake 15 minutes or until pale golden. Cool on trays. Dust with sifted icing sugar, if desired.

COOK'S FILE

Storage time: Dried Fruit Pillows can be kept in an airtight container for up to 4 days.

Knead the dough on a lightly floured surface and form into a ball.

Simmer the fruit mixture until all the liquid has been absorbed.

Fold the pastry over to form a pillow shape and brush tops with egg.

Add egg, juice and rinds to the creamed butter and sugar and beat well.

Turn dough out onto a floured surface and press together until smooth.

LEMON AND LIME BISCUITS

Preparation time: 30 minutes +
  1 hour refrigeration
Total cooking time: 12–15 minutes
Makes 30

150 g butter, softened
3/4 cup caster sugar
1 egg, lightly beaten
1 tablespoon lime juice
2 teaspoons grated lime rind
2 teaspoons grated lemon rind
1 cup plain flour
1/2 cup self-raising flour
60 g marzipan, grated

Lime Icing
1 cup icing sugar, sifted
1 teaspoon finely grated
  lime rind
1 tablespoon lime juice
2 teaspoons water

1 Line two oven trays with baking paper. Using electric beaters, beat butter and sugar in bowl until light and creamy. Add the egg, juice and rinds, beating until well combined.
2 Transfer mixture to a large bowl. Add the flours and marzipan and, using a knife, mix until a soft dough forms. Divide the mixture in two. Turn one portion out onto a lightly floured surface and press together until smooth.
3 Roll biscuit dough into a log shape about 4 cm in diameter. Roll log in plastic wrap and refrigerate 1 hour. Repeat process with remaining dough. Preheat oven to 180°C. Cut dough into 1 cm slices. Place on prepared trays and bake for 10–15 minutes or until lightly golden. Cool on trays.
4 To make Lime Icing: Combine icing sugar, rind, juice and water in a small bowl. Beat the mixture until smooth then either dip biscuits in icing or pipe with an icing bag.

Using a sharp knife, cut each chilled dough log into 1 cm slices.

COOK'S FILE

Storage time: Lemon and Lime Biscuits will keep in an airtight container for up to 4 days.

MELTING MOMENTS WITH JAM AND CREAM

Preparation time: 15 minutes
Total cooking time: 12 minutes
Makes 40

125 g unsalted butter
1/2 cup caster sugar
2 egg yolks
1 teaspoon vanilla essence
1/4 cup custard powder
3/4 cup plain flour
3/4 cup self-raising flour
1/2 cup strawberry jam
3/4 cup thickened cream,
   whipped

1 Preheat oven to 180°C. Line two biscuit trays with baking paper. Using electric beaters, beat butter and sugar until light and creamy. Add egg yolks one at a time, beating thoroughly after each addition. Add vanilla essence; beat until combined.
2 Transfer mixture to a large bowl. Using a flat-bladed knife, incorporate custard powder and sifted flours. Stir until ingredients are just combined. Gather mixture together with fingertips to form a soft dough.
3 Roll 1 level teaspoon of mixture at a time into balls. Arrange about 5 cm apart on prepared trays. Flatten slightly with fork. Bake 12 minutes or until golden. Stand biscuits on trays 5 minutes before transferring to a wire rack to cool. Spread half the biscuits with 1/4 teaspoon jam each. Spoon or pipe cream over jam and sandwich together with remaining biscuits.

COOK'S FILE

Storage time: Store unfilled biscuits in an airtight container for 2 days.

Add egg yolks, one at a time, beating well after each addition.

With your fingertips, gather the biscuit mixture together to form a soft dough.

Arrange biscuits about 5 cm apart on trays and flatten lightly with a fork.

INDEX

Published by Murdoch Books®, a division of Murdoch Magazines Pty Limited,
GPO Box 1203, Sydney NSW 2001.
This flip edition first published in 2003 for Index Books Ltd: Henson Way, Kettering, NN16 8PX, UK

ISBN 1 74045 332 8

CEO: Juliet Rogers **Publisher:** Kay Scarlett. **Food Editors:** Kerrie Ray, Tracy Rutherford. **Editor:** Amanda Bishop. **Designer:** Wing Ping Tong. **Recipe Development:** Wendy Goggin, Michelle Earl, Maria Sampsonis, Jennene Plummer, Janelle Bloom. **Home Economists:** Wendy Goggin, Michelle Lawton, Jo Forrest. **Photographer:** Luis Martin. **Step-by-step Photographer:** Reg Morrison. **Food Stylist:** Mary Harris. **Food Preparation:** Christine Sheppard, Michelle Earl. **UK Consultant:** Maggi Altham

Printed in China by Midas Printing (Asia) Ltd.

Murdoch Books UK Ltd
Ferry House, 51–57 Lacy Road
Putney, London SW15 1PR
United Kingdom
Tel: +44 (0)20 8355 1480
Fax: +44 (0)20 8355 1499
Murdoch Books UK Ltd is a subsidiary
of Murdoch Magazines Pty Ltd.

UK Distribution
Macmillan Distribution Ltd
Houndsmills, Brunell Road
Basingstoke, Hampshire, RG1 6XS
United Kingdom
Tel: +44 (0) 1256 302 707
Fax: +44 (0) 1256 351 437
http://www.macmillan-mdl.co.uk

Murdoch Books®
GPO Box 1203
Sydney NSW 2001
Australia
Tel: +61 (0) 2 8220 2000
Fax: +61 (0) 2 8220 2020
Murdoch Books® is a trademark
of Murdoch Magazines Pty Ltd.